QUIZZES
for
REBEL GIRLS

www.rebelgirls.com

Art director: Giulia Flamini
Cover: Kristen Brittain
Graphics designer: Kristen Brittain
Contributors: Molly Reisner, Sarah Parvis
Special thanks: Grace Srinivasiah, Maithy Vu, Marina Asenjo

Printed in China
First edition, 2022
10 9 8 7 6 5 4 3 2 1

ISBN: 978-1-953424-31-0

3. When Barbara Hillary retired from being a nurse and a taxi driver, she learned to ski and dogsled. She packed up her winter clothes, flew to the Arctic, and skied to the North Pole. How does that sound to you?

Ⓐ That sounds miserable. Too cold and strenuous!

Ⓑ What an adventure! Sign me up!

Ⓒ Hmm. Maybe I could start with a cross-country train trip before I try to ski to the North Pole?

4. You have to do an assignment for school about a famous landmark. What do you pick?

Ⓐ Somewhere I've visited on a class trip. I can describe it better if I've seen it in person.

Ⓑ How about the Eiffel Tower?

Ⓒ Hmm. There are so many amazing options around the world. I'd go online and research everything from Machu Picchu to the Taj Mahal.

5. Loki Schmidt loved plants. She traveled far and wide—from Kenya to the Galapagos Islands—to see rare plant species. She even discovered a new flower in Mexico. Where would you let flowers take you?

A Nearby neighborhood gardens are good for me.

B I'd drive for hours to see a beautiful flower.

C Sign me up for an Amazon excursion. There are new plants to be discovered!

6. Your parents booked a weekend trip to the beach. What do you pack?

A A bunch of bathing suits, lots of outfits to choose from, some books, all of my electronics, and a few of my favorite stuffed animals. Who's in charge of bringing snacks?

B A bathing suit, two outfits, a sweatshirt, and a towel. I can be ready in 15 minutes!

C A backpack with a few changes of clothes and all the essentials

14-18 points

Bon Voyage!

You wild world traveler! You're endlessly curious and not afraid to try out new places or situations. Sushi feasts in Japan, hiking in Honduras, sightseeing in Senegal—it all sounds exciting to you. Get out a globe and pick your dream destination. Maybe you can talk your parents into a trip?

10-13 points

Best of Both Worlds

With plenty of planning, traveling is lots of fun. But you're also happy to stick close to home. Vacation, staycation, you like them both. And when you do go on a trip, you prefer hotels to hiking through the wilderness. Who doesn't love room service?

6-9 points

Happy at Home

Being cozy at home makes for a perfect night. You know what you like, and you're most comfortable when you are surrounded by your own things. When you need to get out and about, there's always the park or your favorite restaurant to visit.

What's Your STEM Style?

1. The school play is coming up. Which of these jobs would you like best?

   A Using chemicals to make fog and other special effects

   B Programming the computer that runs the lighting for the show

   C Building a contraption that makes the sets move

   D Creating a budget and keeping track of all the expenses and ticket sales

2. If you could design one thing, what would it be?

   A An experiment

   B A robot

   C A skyscraper

   D A computer program

3. What would you most want to become famous for?

   A Discovering a new element in the atmosphere

   B Inventing a gadget that translates dog barks into human language

   C Designing the longest bridge in the world

   D Solving an "unsolvable" equation

4. How would you go about building a tree house?

(A) Starting with the stairs, I'd build a few different prototypes, test them out, and then continue with the strongest option.

(B) I'd go online and find a blueprint of a treehouse.

(C) I'd grab some tools and start building. No problem!

(D) I'd draw a plan, mark the measurements, and be careful with the angles as I cut the wood.

5. When you were younger, what were your favorite things to learn about?

(A) Colors

(B) Vehicles

(C) Buildings

(D) Shapes

6. Pick a gadget.

(A) Telescope

(B) Solar-powered car

(C) 3D printer

(D) Kaleidoscope

7. What would you like to learn?

(A) How to use a microscope, like Angella Dorothea Ferguson, whose medical research has saved countless children

(B) How to fly a drone

(C) How to operate a crane

(D) How to use Morse code like Florence Violet McKenzie, who trained hundreds of women during World War II

Answer Key

Mostly As:
Scientist-in-Training

Grab your lab coat! Like Marie Curie, you are ready to use your scientific mind to design clever hypotheses and test them out with even cooler experiments.

Mostly Bs:
Tech Whiz of Tomorrow

Computers and robots and artificial intelligence, oh my! Whether you're bound to design video games, self-driving cars, or 3D-printed tools, tech is your thing. Follow Purva Gupta's lead and test the limits of technology.

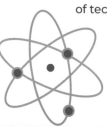

Mostly Cs:
Innovative Engineer

You love to design and build things. Like mechanical engineer Yoky Matsuoka, you'll use your imagination and technical know-how to change the world.

Mostly Ds:
Math on the Brain

Numbers and equations? No problem. Shapes, sizes, and angles? Sure! With your analytical mind, you'd make a great mathematician. Anne-Marie Imafidon might make a marvelous role model.

ARE YOU A MORNING GLORY OR A NIGHT OWL?

To get inspired, painter Carmen Herrera would look out her New York City window and sketch every morning. What kind of landscape would you most like to draw?

Twinkling city lights

A forest on a wintry afternoon

The sun rising on a farm

What group would you join?

Canoeing Club

Astronomy Club

If you worked at a resort, what job would you have?

It's Saturday evening, and you've got a big test on Monday. What's your strategy?

Review half tonight and the rest Sunday evening

Buckle down after Sunday breakfast and study all day

You're on a beach vacation. What's your plan?

Sleep 'til noon. There's no rushing at the beach!

Set my alarm for a morning snorkeling session

When is the best time to eat pancakes?

While watching an evening movie in the family room

With eggs, for breakfast

Run the dance club

Greet guests when they check in

Set up the breakfast buffet

What's your New Year's Eve style?

Take a power nap after lunch and party all night!

Stay up until midnight to watch the ball drop

Do a countdown at 10 p.m., then hit the hay

NIGHT OWL

When the sun goes down, your energy goes up! Would you want to play concerts at night like pop star Madonna?

FEELING FLEXIBLE

Nighttime is great when you've got something fun to do. But like Olympic skater Michelle Kwan, who used to sleep wearing her ice skates, you're also happy to be ready when day breaks.

MORNING GLORY

Like morning glory flowers, you bloom in the a.m. You take a page from sci-fi writer Octavia Butler's schedule. She rose early to write her masterpieces.

What's Your Role in Hollywood?

1. You volunteer to help at an upcoming school dance. What committee do you join?

   A Decorations

   B Music

   C There's no time for committees. I've got to pick my outfit and practice my dance moves!

   D I want to choose the theme.

2. Your birthday is coming up. What surprise gift would you love to receive?

   A A disco ball

   B A pair of headphones

   C A karaoke set

   D A video camera

3. On a road trip, what do you like to do to pass the time?

   A Look out the window

   B Listen to music

   C Share stories with my family

   D Listen to audiobooks. Have you ever listened to stories by Isabel Allende?

4. What's your favorite part of hanging out at the beach?

- (A) Watching the sun set over the water
- (B) Hearing the waves crash along the shore
- (C) Surfing! Swimming! Beach volleyball!
- (D) Climbing into the lifeguard chair for the best view

5. You're rearranging your bedroom. What do you do first?

- (A) Pick the color scheme
- (B) Check to see where the outlets are so I know where to plug in all my electronics
- (C) Decide where the bed and desk go
- (D) Make a drawing of the room, cut out shapes to represent my furniture, and plan the layout

6. What is going on in your head as you read an exciting book?

- (A) I'm picturing all the scenes in my head.
- (B) I'm imagining the voices of each of the characters as they talk.
- (C) I'm thinking about all the cool things my favorite character could do next.
- (D) I'm dreaming up cool ideas for a book I could write.

Answer Key

Mostly As:

A Costume Designer, of Course!

With your eye for colors, fabrics, beauty, and style, costume design would be the right fit for you. Hey, Ruth E. Carter, you did an amazing job with *Black Panther*! Do you need an assistant?

Mostly Bs:

Surely a Sound Designer or Composer

Whether you are working on a movie set or theater stage, you know that music can add so much to any scene. You'd make a stellar sound designer or composer. Like Tania J. León Ferrán, maybe one day you will even conduct your own work.

Mostly Cs:
Absolutely an Actor

Comedy? Drama? Romance? No matter what the story is, you can imagine playing a part. You aren't afraid to get onstage and act your heart out. Like Sophia Loren, you were born to shine on stage or screen!

Mostly Ds:
Definitely a Director

You are great at taking in the big picture and communicating your vision. Plus, you are happy to run the show behind the scenes. Brenda Chapman directed *Brave*. What exciting story would you love to bring to life?

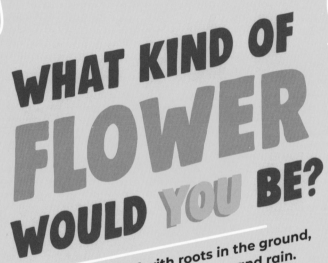

WHAT KIND OF FLOWER WOULD YOU BE?

Imagine yourself with roots in the ground, being nourished by the sun and rain. What type of flower matches you best?

1. Olympic gymnast Gabby Douglas was nicknamed the Flying Squirrel because of how high she flew when she flipped, twisted, and transferred from bar to bar on the uneven bars. What nickname would suit you best?

   A The Colorful Cook. I enjoy making food and sharing it, like chef Pía León does at her restaurants.

   B The Amazing Actor. I want to be in movies like Oscar winner Lupita Nyong'o.

   C The Deep Thinker. I spend time contemplating ideas.

   D The Problem Solver. My friends come to me for advice.

2. Choose a mural for a wall in your room.

   A A stencil with the phrase, "You Got This!"

   B I would draw my own characters, like author-illustrator Beatrix Potter did in her children's books.

   C A surrealist painting, featuring animals and bright colors, in a style like Frida Kahlo's

   D A bold geometric design

3. Peggy Guggenheim loved art and showcased her massive collection in museums. What would you like to collect and exhibit?

   A Smiley face iron-on patches

   B Perfume

   C Crystals

   D Postcards from around the world

4. In the film *Breakfast at Tiffany's*, glamorous actor Audrey Hepburn sips coffee and munches on a pastry in front of a jewelry store. What are you having for breakfast?

A Eggs sunny-side up and some trail mix

B A fruit kebab and French toast

C Oatmeal with lots of brown sugar

D An omelet stuffed with different veggies

5. Pick a dessert.

A Lemon meringue pie

B Red velvet cupcake

C Fresh berries and cream

D A twisty rainbow lollipop

6. What kind of movie do you like best?

A Comedy

B Drama

C Documentary

D Action

7. Eighteenth-century author Jane Austen wrote fictional books about British life as she observed it. What would your book be about?

A A nonfiction book filled with funny jokes and interesting facts

B A mystery with lots of twists and turns

C A story about two friends growing up together

D An autobiography all about my life so far

ANSWER KEY

MOSTLY As: SHINING SUNFLOWER

Tilting your face to the sun like a sunflower, you tap into the warmth and energy of the world around you. Your good spirits are contagious. Like lemonade business founder and bee conservationist Mikaila Ulmer, you care about sustainability and protecting the natural world.

MOSTLY Bs: REGAL ROSE

You may be a bit quiet on the outside, but inside you have a passion that could match opera singer Maria Callas's soulful sound. Just as a rose's thorns protect its delicate leaves, you protect and stand up for others.

MOSTLY Cs: LIVELY LILAC

Lilac bushes are sweet-smelling and hearty. And they can live for 100 years! Now that's a plant that goes the distance—and so do you, especially with your leadership skills. You and climate activist Greta Thunberg both have a knack for rallying support for your causes. What inspires you today?

MOSTLY Ds: DARING DAHLIA

Dahlias come up every year on their own. They're dependable and bright, like you! Your inner strength gives you the confidence to challenge yourself. Journalist Nelly Bly knew a thing or two about a challenge—she broke a world record traveling around the world in less than 80 days.

THE NE
NELLIE
BLY
BEST REPORTER
IN TH

How Do You Speak Your Mind?

Clara Lemlich was a garment worker in the early 1900s. She worked for long hours in a dark, dangerous place, for very little pay. So she took action. If you were being mistreated at work, what would you do?

Suffer quietly and look for a new job

Write a letter to the owner of the company

Organize a strike

You walk into a party full of people you don't know. What's your move?

Help out in the kitchen until my bestie arrives

Introduce myself to a small group that looks friendly

What do you do when you have to give an oral report?

You're at a friend's house for dinner, and fish is on the menu. You don't eat fish. What do you do?

Hide the fish in my napkin and hope I have snacks stashed in my backpack?

Politely let them know I'll stick to the side dishes

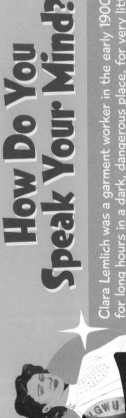

ILGWU

The school play is coming up. Which role do you go for?

The lead! Center stage is the place for me.

Stage crew. I'm a great team player.

Raise my hand to go first

Practice . . . a lot. I'll be a bit nervous but prepared.

Slump down in my seat and hide until the teacher calls on me

How would you help a friend running for class president?

Break out the glitter, it's sign-making time!

Sit with different groups at lunch to spread the word

If you saw a classmate being bullied, what would you do?

Find a teacher or other trusted adult

Check in with the classmate afterward to make sure they're okay

Step up and confront the bully

MARSAI, IS THAT YOU?

You thrive in the spotlight, just like Marsai Martin. You know your mind and are always willing to stand up for yourself and others.

OH HEY, SAMANTHA!

Steady and confident, you know when to stand up and when to hang back. Move over, Samantha Power, there's another diplomat in town!

WHAT'S UP, GEORGIA?

Like Georgia O'Keeffe, you're calm and creative. You find quiet ways to express yourself and show your support.

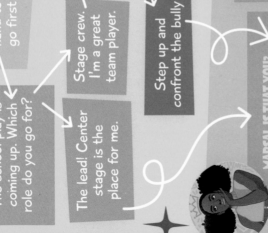

WHAT LIGHTS UP YOUR LEARNING?

1. You're doing a five-minute solo presentation for class. What's your favorite part?

   A Speaking in front of my classmates

   B Writing about what I learned

   C Conducting research

   D Practicing and timing my presentation so I feel ready

2. You've signed up for the talent show. What's your act?

   A Performing a magic trick, ta-da!

   B Reading a short story I wrote

   C Making a homemade volcano erupt

   D Doing a handstand for 30 seconds

3. Pick a poster to put on your wall.

   A Beyoncé—could she be more inspiring?

   B A magical painting of a fantasy world

   C A kitten in a teensy lab coat and safety glasses

   D Olympic gold medal winner BMX cyclist Charlotte Worthington doing a 360 backflip

4. It's a rainy and cold Sunday, and none of your friends are around to play. Bummer! What do you end up doing?

A Whipping up some marvelous muffins, like chef Prue Leith

B Writing a poem about how I'm feeling, like poet Amanda Gorman

C Testing a sample of rainwater for chemicals, like engineer Paige Brown

D Practicing cartwheels, like gymnast Simone Biles

5. Your birthday is coming up, and you get to choose an experience as a present. Cool! What do you decide?

A I'd say yes to an improv class.

B Broadway play, pretty please?

C A trip to the planetarium, of course!

D I want to test my balance at a ropes course.

6. It's your first day at camp and your counselor asks you to describe yourself in three words. Which ones do you choose?

A Social, energetic, expressive

B Thoughtful, creative, observant

C Kind, curious, logical

D Active, funny, competitive

7. What class do you like most?

A Chorus

B Language Arts

C Science

D Gym

Mostly As:
Excellently Expressive

Whether you're acting, singing, dancing, or painting, you're an artist. Like Judith Jamison, you shine when you share your talents with the world. Your ability to express yourself connects you to the world in an important way. The stage is yours!

Mostly Bs:
Rad Writer

Just as novelist Maya Angelou used her storytelling talents to write powerful poems and essays, putting words to a blank page is how you like to express your creative spirit. Getting your thoughts and feelings down on paper helps you learn about yourself and the world. Your words speak volumes. Write on!

Mostly Cs:
Superbly Scientific

Ann Makosinski invented a flashlight powered by body heat, and you're a lot like her. You enjoy observing and exploring the world through science. Making up theories and experiments and then measuring, testing, and recording your findings all light up your magnificent mind. What's your latest discovery?

Mostly Ds:
Fantastically Physical

Whether you're testing out a new trick at the skate park or lacing up your sneakers for an epic tennis match, like Serena Williams, you are dedicated to practicing your moves and getting better each day. Do you dream of competing in the Olympics? Go for it! Train your heart out!

Which Animal Do You Connect with the Most?

In order to train her eagle, Aisholpan Nurgaiv spent time with it. She sang to it, told it stories, and fed it from her hands. After she gained the eagle's trust, they could hunt together. What's your wildlife match?

1. You've got a game night planned. What type of game do you choose?

A A mystery game where I get to solve clues and make decisions

B A game where I can act out words and have an audience

C I like games that aren't too fast and intense. How about a card game, like Crazy Eights?

D If a game is strategic (and I know the rules), then I'm on board.

2. If you could be doing anything right now,
   what would it be?

   A Soaking up vitamin D in the warm sun

   B Tubing down a river with a bunch of buddies

   C Roaming the woods with a good friend

   D Buzzing around the kitchen making a honey cake

3. Adelaide Herrmann dazzled audiences
   worldwide as a magician. Her stage name
   was the Queen of Magic. What noble
   name would you give yourself?

   A Empress of Kickball

   B The Princess of Hilarious Hangouts

   C Your Royal and Loyal Friend

   D The Duchess of Divine Details

4. You're in a TV comedy show.
   What's your character?

   A The can-do main character

   B The bubbly best friend

   C The patient parent

   D The nosy neighbor

5. Chef Asma Khan makes delicious Indian dishes and helps other women start their culinary careers. Now you're in charge of dinner. What's on the menu?

A Let's see, there's meat and veggies in the fridge. I know, beef stew. Let's get chopping!

B Fried fish sandwich . . . I've never made it before, but why not?

C Tacos! Everyone can add the fillings they like best, so we'll all be happy.

D Can we skip straight to dessert? I'll whip up some peach nectar custard bars.

6. It took Jessamyn Stanley's good friend to encourage her to try yoga. She was so nervous! After lots of practice, Jessamyn became a well-known yoga teacher. How do you help your friends?

A I help them tackle a problem right away.

B I use humor to lighten the mood.

C I listen to their problems and help them talk it out.

D I think hard about how I can help, then offer a solution.

7. You're running for mayor. What speech will you make at your next campaign stop?

   A "I promise to get things done and will work nonstop to be the leader you need."

   B "As mayor, I plan on creating a local holiday called Our Town Day, where we celebrate living here in our one-of-a-kind town."

   C "I've lived here my entire life, and this town is a part of me. I promise to listen to our community."

   D "I've got a three-part plan to make our town a more productive and orderly place."

8. Laurie Strand and her daughter Arianna once flew a plane for 12 hours to rescue a frozen pelican. What an adventure! Which adventure would you choose?

   A Being on a show where I could travel the world, competing to win a big prize

   B Visiting somewhere new. I've got a list of countries picked out. But planning out every moment of the trip? No way! I'll wing it!

   C Going to a peaceful cabin in the woods. I'm ready to relax into vacation mode with my family.

   D Learning how to scuba dive from a top-notch instructor

Answer Key

Mostly As: Lion

Lions like you set goals, then smash them. You're confident and bold, like the first Black congresswoman Shirley Chisholm. She was a strong, fearless leader who broke barriers. What's your next goal?

Mostly Bs: Otter

You've got enthusiasm for lots of things and really enjoy talking with your friends. Like Olympic swimmer Ariarne Titmus, your energy is contagious, and you inspire others with what you have to say. When friends need a pick-me-up, who else can give them the perfect pep talk but an outstanding otter?

Mostly Cs: Golden Retriever

Just as pediatric brain surgeon Alexa Canady cares for her young patients, you also care about people and are an amazing listener. Golden retrievers like you have a strong sense of how other people are feeling. That's a superpower called empathy!

Mostly Ds: Honeybee

Honeybees are hard workers, and so are you! No matter what you're doing, you prefer to have a plan of action. You expect the best of yourself and never shy away from a big goal or project. Like Ada Lovelace, the first person to invent a computer program, your ability to think deeper will take you far.

Soaring in Space or Grounded by Gravity?

Starting in the 1950s, photographer Vivian Maier snapped pictures of the reality of everyday street life in US cities. She had a style no one had ever seen before. Picture this: You're behind the camera now. What memorable photo will you be snapping?

A shooting star streaking through the sky

A hot-air balloon festival

Me, midair doing a flip

When you look up at the sky, what do you think about?

The vast universe I can't see beyond the clouds but know is there

How I'm a teensy but mighty speck on Earth

Would you take a once-in-a-lifetime opportunity if it meant leaving your family for a few months?

Which book would you choose?

A history book about the moon landing

A fiction book about a young track star

You have to do an environmental science project. Which topic do you pick?

No, I can do amazing things right where I am.

Plastic litter

Air pollution

Yes! I'd miss them, but I wouldn't want to miss out.

Depends—I'd need to plan for visits back home.

Do you feel claustrophobic in small spaces?

Yes. I wouldn't want to stay in one for long.

You're at an amusement park. Go!

I head to the racetrack for the go-karts. *Vroom!*

I am okay as long as I get breaks.

I rush to the ride that launches me into the air.

No. I can handle them.

GROUNDED BY GRAVITY

You and motocross racer Ashley Fiolek are both ambitious and love the rush of conquering your goals on the ground. Have a rough landing? You've got the grit to get through it!

FLYING HIGH

From high atop a mountain, you see the big picture and are ready to jump into it—like BASE jumper Marta Empinotti! The journey to your goals is all part of your flight to the finish line.

SOARING IN SPACE

You seek new frontiers of experience and knowledge, like astronaut Samantha Cristoforetti. You're a mental space explorer, eager to follow your out-of-this-world ideas.

What Kind of Changemaker Are You?

1. Julia Butterfly Hill once lived in a tall tree for two years to prevent developers from cutting it down. What if the future of your neighborhood nature park was in jeopardy? What would you do?

   A. Organize a sit-in at the park and make a speech about how everyone needs to band together to save it

   B. Write an opinion piece to be published in the local paper

   C. Create flower seed bomb packets for people to toss all around the park

   D. Design and sell T-shirts that say "Love Mother Nature" and donate the money to an organization fighting for the park

2. Inventing a label to help people with visual impairments know when their food has expired, Solveiga Pakštaitė is an example of inclusiveness. How do you make the world a kinder place?

   A. By putting myself in someone else's shoes to understand how they might be feeling

   B. Through the lyrics of my songwriting

   C. By not being wasteful and also by picking up litter whenever I see it

   D. By creating my own plastic-free line of shampoo bars

3. It's Earth Day! How do you honor the planet?

A I'll join a climate movement like Zero Hour, the one activist Jamie Margolin created.

B I'll write a poem about a bee pollinating flowers, like how a young Margaret Atwood wrote about her pet butterfly crawling up her arm.

C I'll plant a garden filled with red flowers and trellises to attract hummingbirds and provide them with lots of tasty nectar.

D I'll start a clothing exchange system with my friends, so we can all share clothes instead of buying new stuff.

4. Your school really needs a new playground. How do you push to make it happen?

A Attend a school board meeting and speak on the issue

B Collaborate with friends to write an original song called "The Recess Blues" and perform it at school

C Give my principal a report with examples of natural materials to use in the new playground

D Ask local businesses to donate to my PTA to help fund the cost

5. Which of these "A" words wins you over?

A Advocate

B Artistic

C Advancement

D Actualize

6. Singer Lady Gaga created a foundation to help spread kindness and give young people a place to talk about mental illness. What would be the focus of your organization?

A. Educating young people on how to be vocal leaders for their causes

B. Launching a website with stories, essays, and poems by young people about issues affecting us today

C. Spreading awareness of sustainable changes everyone can make, like not using plastic straws

D. Creating a fashion line with a positive message, just like empowering designer Kheris Rogers did

7. What kind of summer camp would you go to?

A. An adventure camp where we go on overnight hikes and take turns leading each trek

B. Creative arts camp—I want to act, direct, and produce, like Yara Shahidi.

C. I want to pick my own veggies, collect rainwater, and gather chicken eggs at an environmentally friendly camp.

D. Entrepreneur camp—I've got a business idea I want to grow.

Answer Key

Mostly As: Show-Up Star

When it comes to the causes you care about, you show up. Like wildlife biologist Purnima Devi Barman, who enlisted her community to save a native bird species in India, you have the zest to be an influential leader and changemaker for a better world. What change are you working on?

Mostly Bs: Creative Contributor

You make change through the art you create. Young Jean Lee is a Broadway playwright who writes about complex topics like racism. Whether you are writing, painting, acting, or making films, music, or comedy, you—like Young Jean—hope to engage others and change minds and hearts with your creative expression.

Mostly Cs: Nature Natural

While your connection to the Earth gives you joy, you also recognize the critical importance of doing whatever you can to help the environment. You're inspired by people like Angelina Arora, who used old shrimp shells to create a type of plastic that breaks down quickly and helps plants grow. What Earth-friendly ideas are you brewing?

Mostly Ds: Business Boss

You have a knack for identifying a need (like cold liquids on a hot day for people watching a soccer tournament) and devising a solution (lemonade stand!). Just as entrepreneur Rapelang Rabana made communication more affordable with her internet phone service company, you also plan to use your business brain to improve the lives of others.

TEAM PLAYER ★ OR SOLO STAR?

1. As a child, video game designer Muriel Tramis loved solving crossword puzzles. Now it's your turn to solve one. What's your strategy?

   A Fill in all the answers I know first. Then if I'm stumped, see if someone else can help.

   B Plug away at solving the puzzle on my own, then feel really good when I complete it all by myself.

   C Grab a friend and see if we can tackle it together. We can share in the glory of finishing it.

PLAYER 1 5300

TOP SCORE 10000

2. You're on a camping trip with your family. What's your least favorite part of the trip?

   A Singing the camp songs, stacking the s'mores, mapping out the hikes—I love all of it! (Except maybe my dad's snoring.)

   B Not having much personal space since I'm sharing a tent with everyone. Ugh!

   C Creeping outside to the bathroom in the middle of the night. What if there are bears? Or snakes?

3. Your school is putting on a play. What's your dream role?

A I want to be the director. Like Alice Guy-Blaché, the first female filmmaker, I want to collaborate with the actors and crew to make my vision a reality.

B I'd rather be in charge of the props. I like having a job that's all mine but also requires working with other departments.

C I'd take on a leading role, like Viola Davis. I enjoy the work I do by myself to become my character.

4. What position would you play in soccer?

A Forward. I want to score goals, like Brazilian soccer champion Marta Vieira da Silva did in the Olympics.

B Defense all the way. There's no feeling like kicking the ball away and protecting my goal!

C Center. I love being in the middle of the action, passing the ball back and forth with my teammates.

5. What's your favorite thing on wheels?

(A) A scooter. I can hop on one by myself or scoot around with my neighbors.

(B) A tandem bike. How fun would it be to ride a bike for two with a friend?

(C) Definitely go-karts. Zipping around the track like racecar driver Lella Lombardi pumps me up!

6. What's your favorite way to order at a restaurant?

(A) Family style! I like to share lots of flavors with the table.

(B) I prefer to pick my meal.

(C) Let's split an appetizer and then each choose a main course.

7. Yoshiko Chuma's unique dance choreography and performance style were something audiences had never seen before. If you were on stage, what kind of dance would you do?

(A) I'd bust out my signature break-dancing skills.

(B) I'd do a powerful leap across center stage, then pirouette around with my ballet buddies.

(C) I'd do a precise hip-hop routine that I created with my crew.

17-21 points

Solo Star

You prefer to think on your own and do things your way at your own pace. You're inspired by strong-willed and confident people like motorcyclist Bessie Stringfield, the first Black woman to motorcycle across the United States by herself!

12-16 points

Sometimes in the Spotlight

Sometimes you like making a statement and doing things your way, but you also enjoy being part of a group effort. Soccer player Sarah Fuller, a fierce and focused goalkeeper, is dedicated to her team. Much like her, you know your shining moments are sweetest when others are there to support you.

7-11 points

Team Player

Working together and sharing ideas? Check! Being flexible? Check! What matters most to you are the results of everyone's contributions. Just as the Black Mambas rely on teamwork and communication to protect rhinos from being poached in South Africa, you thrive being one part of a larger effort.

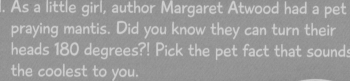

Which Pet Should You Get?

1. As a little girl, author Margaret Atwood had a pet praying mantis. Did you know they can turn their heads 180 degrees?! Pick the pet fact that sounds the coolest to you.

   A This creature has teeth in the back of its throat.

   B This critter chews 200 times a minute, and its teeth never stop growing.

   C This animal can tell when a thunderstorm is coming.

   D This living thing doesn't have a brain but can digest bugs.

2. I want a pet that is . . .

   A . . . low-maintenance but greets me when I come close. I want to keep my pet in my room.

   B . . . energetic and small. I want to play with my pet a lot.

   C . . . smart, furry, affectionate, and playful.

   D . . . unique and really cool to observe.

3. What would you name your pet?

A Goldie

B Piggie

C Whiskers

D Spike

Whiskers

4. As a kid, engineer and entrepreneur Magi Richani constantly took home stray cats and dogs. Caring for your pet is a big part of having one. Which set of tasks can you commit to?

A I will feed my pet every day and change its water twice a week.

B I'll feed my pet a variety of foods, provide fresh bedding and water, clean its cage, and play with it outside of the cage for a few hours every week.

C I will feed my pet on a regular schedule two or three times a day, keep its water fresh, brush it, keep its bathroom clean, and play with it every day.

D I will feed my pet live prey twice a month and make sure it gets lots of sun and distilled water.

5. Every pet requires a certain amount of sleep. Which pet snoozing schedule sounds appealing?

A Sleeps 8 to 12 hours a day, mostly at night; sleeps with eyes open and prefers the dark

B Sleeps 4 hours a day, usually broken into short little naps; often sleeps with eyes open; wakes up easily

C Sleeps 13 to 14 hours a day; is most active at dawn and dusk

D Goes dormant for 10 weeks during winter

6. Pets can be noisy! Which noises are you okay with hearing a lot?

A Soft burbling

B Squeals, tweets, chirrups

C Meows, hisses, growls, purrs

D None!

7. Mealtime! What are you comfortable feeding your pet?

A Sprinkles of food

B Pellets, veggies, hay

C Special cans or packets of meat

D Mealworms and other insects

8. Animals all have their own way of moving. Which pet behavior is your favorite?

A Always moving around

B Jumping up and down like a popcorn kernel ready to pop

C Zooming around and pouncing on toys

D Staying pretty still until it's feeding time

9. As a little girl, Jacinda Ardern, prime minister of New Zealand, had a pet sheep. She tried to train it for a local competition, but it didn't work out so well. Do you want a cuddly pet you can train or one you can admire from a distance?

A I'm okay if my pet isn't made for snuggling. I just want to keep it happy and healthy.

B Petting is great if the animal likes it, but as long as we have some interaction, I will be pleased.

C Bring on the affection! I want a pet that I can hold and stroke.

D No cuddles necessary for me!

Answer Key

Mostly As: Goldfish Wish

Like ballerina Misty Copeland dancing across a stage, goldfish are graceful and mesmerizing to watch as they glide through the water. Plus, they can recognize your face! If you're someone who wants a fairly easy pet to care for, then a goldfish (or two, so they have a buddy) could be right for you.

Mostly Bs: Guinea Pig Glee

With the energy of Nandi Bushell's drumbeats, guinea pigs love to hop around. These sweet companions can be trained to fetch sticks and jump up the stairs. They can be skittish, but your calmness will help them feel safe.

Mostly Cs: Feline Friend

Cats like routines, and so do you. Caring for a kitty would feel natural for you. Like Olympic gymnast Aly Raisman's moves, cats are beautifully coordinated and powerful. They're fun to play games with, and they're fun to watch! A cat is a special friend you can feel close to. What would you name yours?

Mostly Ds: Venus Flytrap

One of a kind, like performer Josephine Baker, Venus flytraps break the mold when it comes to plants. With their teeth-lined leaves, they trap and digest insects and spiders. Venus flytraps may not be furry and affectionate, but they are a marvel of nature, and they need some low-key nurturing to thrive.

What's the Reason for Your Season?

1. What's one new activity you want to try this year?

   (A) Playing ice hockey, like Brigette Lacquette

   (B) Taking a swing at the 18th hole, like golfer Michelle Wie West

   (C) Joining the swim team, like Simone Manuel

   (D) Playing soccer, like Steffi Jones

2. It's evening, and you're ready to chill out. What's the plan?

   (A) Hanging out by the fire, sipping hot cocoa

   (B) Strolling around the block, smelling the flowers

   (C) Swinging on a hammock under the stars

   (D) Making a batch of cinnamon apple muffins

3. Florence Chadwick absolutely loved the sea. She was the first woman to swim both ways across the English Channel. What are your water goals?

   (A) Ice skating

   (B) Watering my herb garden

   (C) Paddleboarding

   (D) Canoeing

52

4. An expert in birds, ornithologist Emilie Snethlage has two birds named after her. One of them is a bright green parakeet that hangs out in loud, chirpy packs. Which type of bird would you like to have named after you?

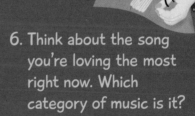

A Penguin

B Songbird

C Flamingo

D Owl

5. Mary, Queen of Scots, had more than 20 dogs and some falcons too! Which animal would you want as a pet?

A A Saint Bernard dog

B A calico kitten

C A bright orange goldfish

D A horse

6. Think about the song you're loving the most right now. Which category of music is it?

A Indie

B Pop

C Oldies

D Rock

7. Wangari Maathai relied on the sun to help the trees she planted grow up tall and healthy. Which sun scenario sounds good to you?

A. Rays reflecting off the snow while I'm sledding down a major hill

B. Feeling the warmth on my arms while I plant flower bulbs in the soil

C. Reading a funny book while I relax under an umbrella at the beach

D. Taking a long walk outside on a crisp, clear day with sunbeams streaming through the tree leaves

8. Fashion designer Diane von Fürstenberg created a popular dress that wraps around the body—with no zippers and no buttons. It was comfortable, easy to throw on, and it looked great on everyone. It's her signature design. What's your signature outfit?

A. Fleece everything!

B. A T-shirt, jeans, and a sweater

C. A tank top and shorts

D. Leggings, a flannel shirt, and a jean jacket

Answer Key

Mostly As: Winter Wonderful

Brrrr, it's cold outside! As a winter person, you value cozy quality time with your loved ones—and the chilly delights winter has to offer too. Snow tubing, anyone? Like mountaineer Poorna Malavath, who climbed Mt. Everest when she was 13 years old, you don't let the snow or cold slow you down!

Mostly Bs: Spring Joy

The butterflies float by, the flowers are blooming, and best of all, it's getting warmer. Surprise, it's spring! Newness and change are all around, and your brain is buzzing like a bee with ideas and creativity. Maybe inventors Ruane and Sheila Jeter need an intern?

Mostly Cs: Summer Fun

The sun shines all day, and you get to play! Whether you're camping, hanging out, hiking, or swimming, you're happy. The freedom and fun that summer offers is 100% you-approved. Ready to catch some waves with surfer Ishita Malaviya?

Mostly Ds: Feeling Fall

The leaves are turning colors and change is in the air. You're ready to learn new things at school and learn new things about yourself. Like Maria Montessori, you appreciate the structure and traditions that fall brings. Classes, extracurriculars, and the upcoming holidays are both comforting and exciting.

WHAT KIND OF MASTERPIECE WILL YOU WRITE?

1. Actor and author Julie Andrews writes children's books with her daughter, Emma. Could you see yourself pairing up with a partner to pen a book?

   (A) I'd create a book of family recipes with my mom, like chef Portia Mbau and her daughter Lumai.

   (B) Yes, my friend can do the drawings.

   (C) I could use someone to read and give me notes, but I'd do all the writing.

   (D) Maybe. Maybe not. Who knows? It's a mystery!

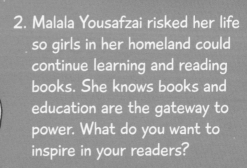

2. Malala Yousafzai risked her life so girls in her homeland could continue learning and reading books. She knows books and education are the gateway to power. What do you want to inspire in your readers?

   (A) A love of taking care of yourself

   (B) A creative spirit

   (C) Confidence in who they are

   (D) Curiosity and excitement

3. A bunch of friends are over, and you're looking for something fun to do. What do you choose?

A Make three different flavors of edible cookie dough and have a taste test

B Sit in a circle and play a storytelling game. I say, "Once upon a time . . ." and make up the first sentence of a story. The person next to me adds a sentence and so on until it's . . . the end.

C Look through old pictures together and reminisce about the cool things we've done

D Go on a scavenger hunt—with cryptic clues and a ticking timer

4. When Nobel Prize-winning author Toni Morrison was young, she was always reading books. Her first novel was called *The Bluest Eye*. What would the title of your first work be?

A *A Memorable Feast*

B *Ava's Time-Traveling Adventure*

C *Me, Myself, and I*

D *The Vanishing of Vera Vallorium*

5. Author Isabel Allende often gets inspiration while she's reading the newspaper. When does inspiration strike for you?

A At the grocery store

B While browsing books at the library

C When I am brushing my teeth and thinking about the day

D Wherever I go, I am always dreaming up "what if" situations. What if there was a spy who . . . ?

6. Your assignment is to write about carrots in any genre you want. What do you write?

A Step-by-step instructions on how to make a carrot cake

B A short story about a girl who ate carrots every day and started to grow a short fluffy tail—with illustrations

C An essay about what I like and dislike about carrots and how they should be served

D A story about how a famous painting of a carrot was stolen

7. Margaret Busby was the first Black female publisher in the UK. She built a respected book publishing company with her business partner. They called it Allison & Busby. What would you name your publishing company?

A Pots & Pans Publishing

B Young Minds Matter Books

C First Person Publishers

D Guess Who? Books

ANSWER KEY

MOSTLY As:

COOKING UP RECIPES

In the kitchen, you dare to dazzle with your distinguished dishes. Like chef and cookbook author Julia Child, you want to share your best tried-and-true recipes with the world. Maybe you'll whip up a breakfast cookbook? Or are desserts your thing?

MOSTLY Bs:

CHILDREN'S BOOKS

Some of your favorite books are the ones you read when you were little. Creating new characters and worlds with your words and drawings is how you express your imagination. Check out Astrid Lindgren's Pippi Longstocking books.

MOSTLY Cs:

MEMORABLE MEMOIR

Writing the stories and emotions of your life gives you the space to explore any moment of your life in more depth. Just as Mary Seacole wrote about being a nurse in the 1800s, you can express your feelings about the world as well.

MOSTLY Ds:

TWISTY MYSTERIES

You'll use the power of words to stir up all kinds of mischief and trickery when you write your head-scratching whodunits. Like mystery book master Agatha Christie, you construct a puzzling plot that's hard to solve but super fun to try. What clues are you concocting?

ARE YOU A CREATURE OF HABIT?

1. Katrina Lake started an online fashion business that helps people buy clothes they feel good in. It's Pajama Day at school tomorrow, and you get to wear pjs to class. Which ones do you choose?

   Ⓐ Hmmm . . . I'll decide in the morning.

   Ⓑ A fresh pair of plaid flannels, already laid out on my dresser

   Ⓒ Either my rainbow-striped pajama pants or the galaxy ones—I'll see what mood I'm in when I wake up.

2. It's dinnertime at your favorite restaurant. You order:

   Ⓐ The special—I've never had it before and it sounds tasty!

   Ⓑ My usual drink, entrée, and dessert. That's what I came for.

   Ⓒ Some new appetizers and the tried-and-true spaghetti.

62

3. Architect Lina Bo Bardi designed an amazing art museum in Brazil. It looks like a glass rectangle floating above the ground with two hefty red pillars holding it up. For homework, you need to design a structure with toothpicks and marshmallows that will support a book on top of it. What's your process?

A Research which shapes are the strongest, map out each step on paper (including how many supplies I'll need), then start building

B Experiment with different structures, testing each step along the way

C Start building and use my intuition as a guide

4. Léopoldine Doualla-Bell Smith, the first Black flight attendant, has flown into airports all over the globe. You're at the airport about to go on a family vacation when your flight gets delayed for four hours. What do you do?

A Relax into a good book

B Go on an impromptu scavenger hunt to pass the time

C Think about how this affects the rest of the day's activities

5. In studying chimpanzees, Jane Goodall discovered that, like humans, they have their own rituals. What special ritual would you do to feel lucky?

A If the clock says 11:11 or 3:33, I make a wish.

B There's a four-leaf clover inside the locket I wear. I kiss the locket for luck when I need it.

C I wear my lucky socks (if I remember).

6. You come home from school and see that someone has rearranged the living room furniture. How do you feel?

A Upset

B Excited

C Curious

7. Explorer Mary Kingsley was the first woman to climb Mount Cameroon in Africa. What's the most adventurous thing you'd do?

A There's parasailing at a nearby beach. I won't stop begging until my parents let me try it.

B I'll gather up my courage and dive off the high dive at the pool.

C Sharing a cabin with my best friend at sleepaway camp sounds like a wild time!

17-21 POINTS

SUPER SPONTANEOUS

When snowboarding champion Chloe Kim was little, her dad drove through the night so they could snowboard as the sun came up. That's the kind of trip you would sign up for! In pursuing new experiences, you don't overthink every decision because when you go with your gut, you feel true to yourself. What memories will you make next?

12-16 POINTS

ALL ABOUT BALANCE

Atop a high wire, acrobat Madame Saqui stunned the circus audience with her agility and balance. You're also terrific at balancing—and balancing the pros and cons of whatever situation you're in. You relish your routines but are also game to try something out of the ordinary. What's the last unexpected thing you've done?

7-11 POINTS

PERPETUAL PLANNER

Eileen Gray, architect and furniture designer, drew the blueprint for her villa house and designed all the furniture inside. That took some major planning, which is something you know a lot about! You take pride in preparation and comfort in routine. When Plan A doesn't work out, that's okay. You've already got Plans B, C, and D in mind. A disruption in your routine can be tough, but hey, you'll just find a new one that works.

Which Body of Water Would You Be?

1. When ocean advocate Danni Washington was little, she spent every possible moment swimming in a pool. Are you a swimmer too? Picture yourself at a waterpark. Which section do you visit first?

   A The wave pool

   B The regular pool

   C The newest water ride

   D The wet zone—where giant buckets of water rain down on me

2. Travel guides Valentina Quintero and her daughter Arianna cohosted a TV show about their explorations in Venezuela. If you were to travel there, which wonder of water would you want to wade in?

   A The Caribbean Sea

   B Lake Maracaibo

   C Orinoco River

   D Angel Falls—the tallest waterfall in the world!

3. When you're feeling bored, how do you pass the time?

(A) I write in my journal.

(B) I call a friend.

(C) I find fun things to do. Did you know that if you walk around the house while looking down into a mirror, it looks like you are walking on the ceiling?

(D) I build a fort.

4. Which word or phrase describes you the least?

(A) Open book

(B) Social butterfly

(C) Boring

(D) Calm

5. Singer-songwriter Taylor Swift once arrived at an awards show in a horse-drawn carriage. How do you make an entrance?

(A) With a wave hello

(B) Quietly

(C) I flow in gracefully

(D) With a statement!

6. When math whiz Anne-Marie Imafidon was young, she used her creativity to build websites. You feel most creative when you . . .

A . . . write a story about a mysterious mermaid.

B . . . paint a still life of a pet turtle.

C . . . learn something new, like juggling.

D . . . are trying out scenes in improv class.

7. Susan Francia started rowing in college. And she immediately felt her confidence and determination grow. Later, she won two Olympic gold medals for rowing! What's the coolest thing to do on the water?

A Boogie board

B Kayak

C Go rafting

D Jump into it

Answer Key

Mostly As: Ocean Motion

Like the ocean, you have many layers. Sometimes you're fun and playful. Other times, you go deep and quietly explore your thoughts. You can be more than one thing, like Hedy Lamarr, who was both an actor and an inventor. Just as you can count on the waves crashing on the shore, others can count on you to be a good friend.

Mostly Bs: Like a Lake

The peaceful surface of a lake is calm and friendly, and so are you! Like veterinarian and conservationist Gladys Kalema-Zikusoka, who protects endangered animals, your connection to nature and your compassionate heart make you caring and kind.

Mostly Cs: River Rider

Is anything more relaxing than inner tubing down a river? You ride life's currents with a questioning mind that's ready for adventure, like French explorer Jeanne Baret. The rush of the river excites your senses. Where will the current take you?

Mostly Ds: All Waterfall

Waterfalls are magical wonders of water. Don't you think? They also capture a lot of attention—something you do not shy away from. You draw an audience with your natural charisma and heart of gold, like Argentine politician Evita Perón did for her country's people. A waterfall shimmers and shines like you!

PATIENT OR PERPETUALLY RESTLESS?

Mathematician Maryam Mirzakhani once said, "The beauty of mathematics only shows itself to more patient followers." What have you accomplished through practicing patience?

Does waiting for my brownies to bake count?

Waiting for the coach to put you in the soccer game, you:

Pace on the sidelines, wanting to play

Strategize how you'll play best

After weeks of training him, my dog can do new tricks!

What would you do if the book you just started reading isn't drawing you in?

I grew out my hair for a year so I could donate it.

Your dad said he'd take you to a friend's house, but he's still on the phone. What do you do?

Hover nearby, interrupting him every few minutes

Write a note asking him how long he will be

Your leg is broken, and it's hard to move. What do you do?

→ Yell for help anytime I want something.

Grab a different book. It's not a match, so I will move on.

→ Try to do as much as I can on my own

Skim through the entire book to see if it gets more interesting

Microwave lasagna

What meal would you make?

Scrambled eggs and toast

Give it three more chapters and then reassess

Check the contest website 10 times a day

Spaghetti with homemade meatballs

You entered a writing contest. What do you do while waiting for the results?

Start a new piece for another contest

WORKING ON IT

Motivation paired with patience is key. Ursula Burns became a CEO by setting big picture goals and logging in years of hard work. Practice mindfulness when you're feeling antsy for action!

PRETTY PATIENT

Like mushroom farmer and educator Chido Govera, you reap the rewards of investing yourself in your goals. Your calm nature brings peaceful vibes wherever you go.

PATIENCE PERFECTED

When ice diver Johanna Nordblad swims beneath a frozen lake, she must practice total control to stay safe. Have you noticed that when you're in control and patient, you have better outcomes?

What Kind of Science Speaks to You?

1. It's Facts Friday at school, and it's your turn to share an interesting fact with the class. Which one do you choose?

    A Indonesia has the most volcanoes in the world.

    B Strawberries are the only fruit with seeds on the outside.

    C The most ancient life-form we know is bacteria. They're more than 3.5 billion years old.

    D An ichthyologist is a scientist who studies fish.

2. How would you use your scientific mind to make the world a better place?

    A I'd like to study all the different types of rocks that can be found around the world.

    B I want to research the medicinal qualities of plants to find out how they can heal people.

    C I want to develop vaccines to protect people from viruses.

    D I'd like to work with local communities to conserve their natural wildlife.

3. Using her microscope for research, geneticist **Nettie Stevens** discovered that chromosomes determine whether an animal is born male or female. If you had a microscope, what would you want to study?

(A) The minerals in the soil

(B) The structure of different types of leaves

(C) The mold growing on old cheese in the fridge

(D) A shedded snakeskin

4. It's field trip day at the science museum! What exhibit are you most excited about?

(A) The display of pillow lavas from an undersea volcano

(B) A walk through a greenhouse jungle

(C) The enlarged photographs of microscopic viruses. They look so cool it is hard to imagine how they make people sick!

(D) The live animal habitats

5. Marine biologist Sylvia Earle spent weeks living underwater, exploring and researching sea life. She even touched the bottom of the ocean! What expedition would you go on?

A I'd take a trip to see the active volcano Mount Stromboli in Italy.

B I'd go on a journey to Madagascar to explore the rare spiny forests.

C I'd visit a microbe-making company and learn how bacteria is used to make foods like yogurt.

D I'd work at a wild elephant conservation park in Sri Lanka.

6. Fascinated by the teeny particles that make up an atom, physicist Sau Lan Wu devoted her research to discovering more about atoms. What is something in the natural world that fascinates you?

A Way beneath our feet, deep underground, is the Earth's outer core. It is filled with hot, liquid rock.

B Plants have their own form of intelligence. They can communicate with one another.

C Algae make most of the oxygen on the planet.

D Octopuses are incredibly smart. They can open jars to get the food inside.

7. In her lab, neuroscientist Daniela Schiller conducts experiments about how brain chemistry works. You probably don't have access to a lab like Daniela does, so which at-home experiment would you try?

A Mixing baking soda and vinegar to cause a chemical reaction

B Placing a clear plastic bag over different plants to see how much water is released from their leaves

C Making a naturally glowing lamp using bioluminescent microbes

D Building a bird feeder with four separate feeding stations and filling it with four different types of seeds to learn which birds like each type of seed

Answer Key

Mostly As:
Very Much a Volcanologist

When it comes to volcanoes, you dig deep into learning about Earth's rocky layers and fiery core. Just as volcanologist Katia Krafft had a passion for the drama and excitement of lava explosions, you too get thrills from watching active eruptions.

Mostly Bs:
Born for Botany

Plants aren't just there in the background. For you, they're the main attraction! Scientist Ameenah Gurib-Fakim felt that plants were like friends, and you do too. As a botanist, you hope to contribute to a future where plants are respected for their priceless role in the environment.

Mostly Cs:

Microbiologist to the Max

Microbiology is the study of microbes—tiny organisms you can't see without a microscope, like viruses and bacteria. Roseli Ocampo-Friedmann used her science skills to grow rare microbes in her lab for research. With your analytical and curious mind, perhaps you'll even pioneer a vaccine!

Mostly Ds:

Zest for Zoology

Since your connection to animals is so strong, you'd use your caring and determined scientific spirit to help protect animal habitats. For you, preserving wildlife is crucial for Earth's future. Would you have a pet Komodo dragon like zoologist Joan Beauchamp Procter?

What Business Will You Start?

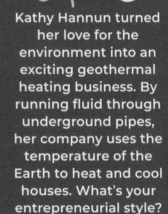

Kathy Hannun turned her love for the environment into an exciting geothermal heating business. By running fluid through underground pipes, her company uses the temperature of the Earth to heat and cool houses. What's your entrepreneurial style?

1. How would your business contribute to the community?

A It would create jobs.

B We would offer advice to other business owners.

C I would source the ingredients for my business from nearby farms.

D It would provide services that help decrease waste.

2. In your business, what experience do you want your customers to have?

   A To feel confident, like fans of Rihanna's Fenty Beauty products

   B To feel supported, like the companies Aileen Lee supports with startup money

   C To feel satisfied, like the diners at Leah Chase's restaurant

   D To feel empowered to help the Earth, like Julie Chen's customers feel when they use her bamboo paper products

3. Melanie Perkins's company motto is "Empowering the world to design." What would your company's motto be?

   A "Feel Good and Look Good!"

   B "Growing Connections"

   C "Taste Happy"

   D "Planet Approved"

4. You received $100 for your birthday! What do you plan on doing with it?

A Buying fabric for a jumpsuit I want to sew

B Putting it in my savings account and watching it grow

C Purchasing mason jars for my homemade pickles

D Signing up for a beekeeping class

5. Brazilian entrepreneur Adriana Barbosa organized an outdoor shopping market called Feira Preta. Vendors sold all sorts of things there—headscarves, natural beauty products, shoes, toys, crafts, and more. Imagine you are walking through her bustling market. What stalls would you like to check out?

A The body soaps and lotions stand

B All of them!

C The food trucks

D The ones filled with vintage stuff

6. In the late 1800s, Margarete Steiff founded a toy company and named it after herself. Another founder, Mar Hershenson, and her business partner named their company Pear VC. Why did they pick pear? Because "pear trees stand out as being strong, long-lived, and hearty." Pear also sounds like *pair*, and the company was formed by a powerful pair of investors. What would your company name be?

    A Knock-Knock Socks (socks with knock-knock jokes on them!)

    B Seed Investments

    C Big Sips Beverages

    D Happy Soil

7. What traits do you have that will help you start a business?

    A My unique vision, hands-on approach, and people skills make me a good leader.

    B I make good decisions and can assess situations well.

    C I'm motivated, like to experiment, and am open to feedback.

    D I'm caring, good at planning, and can come up with efficient solutions to fix problems.

Answer Key

Mostly As:
Beauty and Fashion Guru

Whether it's mixing up your own lip gloss or repurposing pants as shorts, you take pride in how you present yourself. Like jewelry CEO Noura Sakkijha, your ambitious creativity will have you serving up looks that your customers will crave. What fresh designs are you drawing up today?

Mostly Bs:
Venture Capitalist

Opportunity knocks for a venture capitalist! Investor Arlan Hamilton invests money in companies she believes in to help them grow. You also have a talent for tapping opportunities by being engaged with those around you. And you like being part of different projects—it's exciting!

Mostly Cs: Tastemaker

Do you like making yummy food and sharing it? Tastemakers literally make taste! Just as chef Daniela Soto-Innes creates a joyful community in her restaurants, you'd also bring warmth and fun to your food business. What tasty flavors will you be stocking up on?

Mostly Ds: Sustainable Specialist

When it comes to helping Earth, you lean green. You're paying attention to the environment and learning from people like Hu Weiwei. When pollution got bad in her city, she created a bike-sharing company to lower car use and gas emissions. What sustainable business will you build?

Resilient or Resigned?

1. Uh-oh! Your dog just ate your homework—literally. It took a long time to finish, and it's due tomorrow. What do you do?

   A. Feel overwhelmed and discouraged, flop on the couch, and watch a TV show

   B. Shake off being upset, take many deep breaths, then redo the work

   C. Scream into a pillow, do half the assignment, and hope the teacher will give you more time when she hears your tale of puppy woe

2. Ballerina Alicia Alonso lost her vision when she was an adult. She had to overcome many obstacles in order to dance again. She was even bedridden for a whole year! Would you keep going after your goal, even if it got really hard?

   A. For sure! No matter how tough things get, I go after my goals.

   B. Maybe. I might reconsider my plans.

   C. No. What's the point when there are so many obstacles?

84

3. You're running at your track meet and can see the finish line . . . and the six competitors in front of you. What are you thinking?

A. "I wish I wasn't so slow! Oh well, there's always next time."

B. "There's no way I'm going to win. They're faster than me."

C. "I'm going to push my hardest no matter what—like Olympic runner Wilma Rudolph."

4. Your family is moving across the country for a new job. For you, that means there will be a new, well, everything. How do you think this change will be for you?

A. Hard, but I have no choice, and I'll just have to see what happens.

B. Tough, but I'm going to make the best of it even if it's uncomfortable for a while.

C. Impossible! I'll never make as good friends as the ones I have now. I wish I could stay where I am!

5. Oops! You accidentally broke a special dish at home. What do you do?

Ⓐ Freak out, stash it in my closet, and hope no one notices

Ⓑ Offer to glue it back together

Ⓒ Feel guilty, keep it to myself for a few hours while looking online for replacements, then confess

6. Your best friend is spending more time with someone who isn't you. This makes you sad. What do you do?

Ⓐ Invite her over and let her know how much I miss her

Ⓑ Avoid eye contact with her and assume she's mad at me

Ⓒ Wait to see if she reaches out first, and if she doesn't, then I'll make the effort

7. You are at the beach when all of a sudden—*splash!*—a big wave topples the giant sandcastle you've been working on all morning. You were just about to take a picture of it! An hour later, how do you feel?

Ⓐ Still frustrated. I spent so much time on it!

Ⓑ A little annoyed. I really wanted a picture to send to my friends.

Ⓒ Like I want to build another one, but this time, I will build farther away from the shoreline.

17–21 points

Resigned (for Now)

Do you feel a little helpless when things don't go your way? When singing sensation Gloria Estefan got into an accident, she worked hard to get back on stage. To be resilient like Gloria, set realistic goals and promise yourself you'll meet them. When you do, celebrate your growth!

12–16 points

Extra Effort Required

Sometimes you need a little push in order to move past your obstacles. But once you commit to trying, you're unstoppable. Activist Manal al-Sharif helped make it legal for women to drive in her country. Take the steering wheel like Manal and navigate toward your goals.

Bouncing Back

7–11 points

As an ultramarathoner, Lowri Morgan runs through extreme conditions, like the Amazon jungle and the Arctic! Pushing through your challenges is something both you and Lowri do. You know there'll be ups and downs, but your goals are worth the journey it takes to get there.

WHAT IS YOUR SUPERPOWER?

1. **How do you cheer up your friends when they're feeling blue?**

   (A) Improvise a silly dance to their favorite song

   (B) Just be with them and listen

   (C) Get them out of their head and into action by doing something like going for a bike ride or throwing a Frisbee

   (D) Share something new with them. Maybe we could try orange-flavored chocolate?

2. **You were recently voted most likely to . . .**

   (A) . . . perform on Broadway.

   (B) . . . work in the White House.

   (C) . . . compete at the World Championships.

   (D) . . . invent something amazing.

3. **Which one of these activities could you imagine doing?**

   (A) Rapping in front of an audience, like MC Soffia did at the Olympics

   (B) Organizing a climate strike, like activist Xiye Bastida

   (C) Sprinting in a race, like Olympian Florence Griffith Joyner

   (D) Sailing on the high seas, like pirate Grace O'Malley

4. Your school is doing an auction and needs items and services for people to bid on. What would you contribute?

A A recording of a customized song, written for the highest bidder

B A Buddy Bench for the playground. If someone sits there, it means they'd like to meet a new friend.

C A jump-roping lesson, where I share all my best techniques and tricks

D A local guidebook of not-so-well-known places to explore in my neighborhood

5. Erica Armah Bra-Bulu Tandoh was a little girl when she discovered DJing. By the time she was nine years old, she was on stage spinning records at parties, making the crowd smile and dance. She's now known as DJ Switch Ghana. What do you like to do at parties?

A I like to play games like Make Me Laugh— where you try to make another person laugh without laughing yourself.

B I like to get everyone out on the dance floor.

C Doing flips on the trampoline is super fun for me!

D I like to come up with brand-new games to play.

6. Costume designer Ruth E. Carter makes superhero costumes for movies. If you were designing a new superhero suit for yourself, what symbol would you put on your cape?

A A microphone

B A heart

C A lightning bolt

D A rocket ship

7. When Carmen Amaya danced flamenco, she wore men's clothes. The crowd didn't like that—they expected her to wear a dress. Carmen didn't budge, and her fans eventually accepted her style. What challenges have you had to overcome in order to be yourself and do things your own way?

A I've learned to calm my jittery nerves before performing.

B I've had to work on my fear of standing up for others.

C I'm getting better at staying confident when I don't meet my goals.

D I'm training myself to get past a slump when I don't feel inspired.

ANSWER KEY

MOSTLY As:

STAGE PRESENCE

Your superpower is the magnetic creative presence you share with an audience. Whether you're giving it your all with your acting or captivating your friends with a karaoke performance, like the singer Insooni, you leave the crowd wanting more!

MOSTLY Bs:

STANDING UP FOR OTHERS

Caring about how others feel and working to protect the environment are some of the ways your superpower shines. Just as sisters Ella and Caitlin McEwan petitioned fast-food companies to stop giving away ocean-polluting plastic toys, you too can inspire others to take action.

MOSTLY Cs:

SPEEDY AND STRONG

Warp speed ahead! You've dedicated time and effort to your impressive physical feats. The mental strength to push yourself is your superpower. Luo Dengping is an extreme rock climber in China who forged her own path in what was considered a man's sport. Like Luo, your determination will keep you reaching new heights.

MOSTLY Ds:

EAGER EXPLORER

Mary Anning was a self-taught paleontologist who discovered a 30-foot-long fossil of an ancient reptile near her home. Mary didn't need to travel far to make a discovery, and neither do you. Whether it's exploring a nearby town or trying a new food, your superpower is allowing your curiosity to lead the way.

Confident or Conflicted?

When Senegalese model Khoudia Diop was growing up, people tried to make her feel inferior for having dark skin. To squash the negativity, she would look in the mirror and tell herself, "You are beautiful." What are your confidence-boosting habits?

Hmmm, I don't have any yet.

I spend time with good friends.

I remind myself of my victories.

You're invited to a party where you know only one person. Do you go?

Sure (though I'd feel a little nervous)

No way. What if no one talks to me?

In the middle of your dance recital, you forget part of the routine. What are you doing onstage?

At school, a classmate tells you in front of others that you've got lettuce stuck in your teeth. How do you react?

With my cheeks burning from embarrassment, I'd rush to the bathroom.

I'd crack a joke and thank them for the heads-up.

In a class discussion, you have an idea to contribute. Do you share it?

Yes, I like participating!

If I feel like it's definitely, 100%, a good idea

Moving and pretending I know what I'm doing. Big smile!

Freezing for a few seconds, then trying to follow along

Booking it offstage in a panic

In math class, you got a bad grade on a test. How do you deal with a setback?

Figure I'm not good at math and hope the next test will be easier

Ask the teacher for extra help so I understand what I got wrong

You overhear a school acquaintance make fun of your outfit. What do you do?

Feel ashamed and vow never to wear the outfit again

Flip-flop between feeling bad about the comment and mad at the person who said it

Stand tall and refuse to let someone else's negative opinion ruin my day

KIND OF CONFLICTED

Feeling like you're good enough or that you belong takes practice! Try seeing challenges as a path to growth and make your next move, like chess champion Phiona Mutesi.

MIXED EMOTIONS

Do you sometimes feel like you're on top of the world, and other times, not so much? That's normal! Like ballerina Michaela DePrince says, "Never be afraid to be a poppy in a field of dandelions."

FULLY CONFIDENT

Like billiards pro Karen Corr, you keep taking your shots even when the odds are against you. Your confidence comes from not comparing yourself to others and staying true to yourself!

What Color Matches Your Spirit?

1. You have a ticket to anywhere in the world! Where are you headed and why?

    (A) Straight to the Swiss Alps for skiing

    (B) "Down under," so I can explore sunny Australia

    (C) To Japan, where I can meander through magical forests

    (D) Off to Belize to snorkel in the sparkling water

2. Fashion influencer Meryem Slimani uses her eye for pattern and color to take exciting pictures of her mother that aim to inspire. You're working on a collage of pictures that inspire you. What are three images you would add?

    (A) A family photo, a shot of Mt. Everest, and a picture of a pizza

    (B) A photo of a field of tulips, a picture of me kneeling in a human pyramid with my friends, and a thumbs-up emoji

    (C) A picture of a monarch butterfly, the pi symbol, and a shot of a rocket launch

    (D) Photos of a double rainbow, my dog, and my favorite singer

3. You and three classmates are tasked with writing and presenting a report about blizzards. What strengths do you bring to a group assignment?

A. Leading and delegating work, like editor-in-chief Anna Wintour does at her magazine job

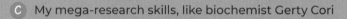

B. Bringing my can-do attitude, like Kristal Ambrose does. She gathered young people together to convince the Bahamian government to ban single-use plastics.

C. My mega-research skills, like biochemist Gerty Cori

D. Staying calm, like fighter pilot Thokozile Muwamba

4. Mother-daughter duo Briana and Cambyr Sullivan hiked the entire Appalachian Trail together. That's 2,000 miles! Now it's your turn to hike the trail. What's one thing you're bringing along?

A. My phone so I can share my progress with my friends

B. A harmonica to play at night by the fire

C. Binoculars to see wildlife

D. A bathing suit so I can take dips in the water along the way

5. In high school, computer scientist Timnit Gebru was discouraged by a teacher who didn't think she could handle advanced classes because she was an immigrant. But she focused on physics and math, aced her classes, and earned a spot at a top university. What do you do when you feel discouraged?

A   I thrash around my room and pound my bed, and then I feel better.

B   I talk to a friend. That usually gets me back into a positive mindset.

C   I ride my bike and let the negative feelings drift away.

D   I have a heart-to-heart with my cat. She always knows how to comfort me.

6. The Cholita Climbers are a group of Indigenous women in Bolivia who defy expectations and hike up snowy mountains in their bright skirts. How do you challenge others to think differently?

A   I joined a team where I'm the only girl.

B   Instead of getting birthday presents, I ask for donations to an animal shelter.

C   I eat food grown locally to help the planet.

D   I purposely became friends with someone at school who didn't have any.

Answer Key

Mostly As: Rock That Red

Olympic ice hockey player Geraldine Heaney didn't let the naysayers who said girls can't play hockey stop her. You share Geraldine's determined spirit. Colored red, your spirit is full of the energy you put into making your goals a reality and keeping your friendships strong.

Mostly Bs: Hello Yellow

Giselle Burgess founded Girl Scout Troop 6000, a chapter for homeless girls so they could be part of a loving community. Like Giselle, you paint the world yellow with a hopeful spirit and acts of kindness. You and your friends can count on each other to listen and care.

Mostly Cs: Going Green

Whatever you're up to, your harmonious spirit makes everyone around you feel at ease—that's the calming power of green working its magic! Lina and Sanna El Kott Helander, sisters who win races running up mountains, share your love of exploring the world and leading with curiosity.

Mostly Ds: Blast of Blue

When in nature, your blue spirit blossoms. Like sailor Jessica Watson, you're especially drawn to the mysterious blue waters of oceans. You think a lot about what contribution you will make to the world and how you'll help improve it with your compassionate heart. That's the blue in you!

What Kind of Queen Would You Be?

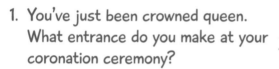

1. You've just been crowned queen. What entrance do you make at your coronation ceremony?

   A On a golden barge, adorned with jewels and silk, like Cleopatra

   B Belting out a victory song, like Queen of Soul Aretha Franklin

   C With a special sash and gown, like pageant queen Zozibini Tunzi

   D Vrooming down the aisle on my bike, like the Motorcycle Queen of Miami Bessie Stringfield

2. An opposing force is threatening your position as queen! What would you do?

   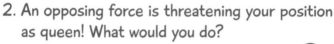

   A Fight them in court, and if that doesn't work, assemble my army

   B Rally people together with powerful speeches and songs about unity

   C Offer a peaceful meeting with a treaty to sign

   D Challenge them to an Olympic-style contest

3. As queen, what would you wear during public events?

(A) My crown and an elegant gown or suit

(B) An eye-catching outfit that I can dance around in

(C) A shirt with a message of equality and love

(D) An ensemble that expresses who I am and how I am feeling that day

4. Nefertiti, Queen of Egypt in 1300s BCE, changed how people prayed. Instead of worshipping many gods, she prayed to one, Aten the sun god. As queen, what new rule are you declaring?

(A) All people shall be treated equally.

(B) There shall be countrywide music festivals every weekend.

(C) Everyone shall help their community one day a month.

(D) All schools shall be free.

5. What does your castle look like?

A A solid, well-protected compound built on top of a steep hill, like Matilda of Canossa's castle in the Middle Ages

B A welcoming place filled with comfort food, cozy couches, and marvelous music

C My castle is my home, where I plan to make an impact on the world!

D I designed my castle to suit my unique taste, like architect and Queen of the Curve Zaha Hadid.

6. How would you create a positive message to promote to your people? I would . . .

A . . . support the development of arts and literature, like Queen Elizabeth I did.

B . . . write and sing a new national anthem celebrating love and kindness.

C . . . lead by example as someone who fights for human rights.

D . . . provide opportunities for everyone to explore their passions.

7. After her royal father died, Queen Christina of Sweden became a queen when she was just six years old. How would you become queen?

(A) It's my legacy.

(B) The people deemed my entertainment skills to be worthy of the title.

(C) I stood out as a leader in my community.

(D) I'm one of a kind in my field.

Answer Key

Mostly As:

Queen of the Land

Hear ye, hear ye! A new queen is about to ascend the throne, and with her brilliant leadership and clever strategy, the country will flourish and prosper. Her name is . . . YOU! Like Empress Taytu Betul of Ethiopia, you would fight on the front lines to keep your citizens safe and free.

Mostly Bs:

Queen of the Band

Your scepter is a microphone, the band is your court, and your power comes from the stirring lyrics you sing to the crowd! With her beautiful voice and sizzling stage presence, singer Celia Cruz was nicknamed the Queen of Salsa. What music genre will you rule?

Mostly Cs:

Queen of Taking a Stand

Transgender activist Marsha P. Johnson, known as the Queen of the Village in New York City, fought hard for LGBTQIA+ rights. Just as Marsha dedicated her life to protecting others, your compassion compels you to lead with your heart.

Mostly Ds:

Queen of My Own Brand

Your unique and exciting vision for how you see and interact with the world is something to behold! Like the Queen of Kona, triathlete Paula Newby-Fraser, and the Queen of Talk, Oprah Winfrey, you strive for excellence and growth in everything you do.

How Do You Like to Move Your Body?

1. It's a gorgeous day outside. Hooray! What are you doing outside?

   A Walking to the stream in the woods near my house to see if there are any salamanders

   B Cruising around the block on my hoverboard

   C Meeting up with my team for softball practice

   D Swimming in my friend's pool

2. Homework break! What do you do?

   A Head to the backyard to watch a rabbit nibble on the grass

   B Hop on the stationary bike to burn some energy

   C Practice martial arts like Keiko Fukuda

   D Pump some iron, like weightlifter María Isabel Urrutia

3. What's one new thing you want to learn?

A Geocaching. High-tech scavenger hunts sound awesome.

B How to unicycle

C To play lacrosse

D I want to learn spelunking, so I can explore caves.

4. Feeling energetic? Pick an afternoon activity.

A Go on a nature walk and collect leaves, twigs, rocks, and acorns to make some crafts

B Dress up in retro style and go roller-skating for '80s night

C Play a game of freeze tag with my friends

D Practice my dance moves in the mirror

5. Munchie time! Name your favorite part about making chocolate chip cookies (besides eating them).

A The energy boost I get from sampling chocolate chips

B Using the electric mixer

C Scooping out the raw dough and dropping it into neat rows

D Cracking the eggs

6. **You're at a recreational park with lots of options for activities. Pick one.**

   Ⓐ Follow a trail and hike through the forest

   Ⓑ Paddleboating, pronto!

   Ⓒ Kickball with a big group

   Ⓓ I want to try zip-lining!

7. **How do you wind down before you climb into bed?**

   Ⓐ A few minutes of stretching soothes my muscles.

   Ⓑ I watch Sky Brown skateboarding videos.

   Ⓒ I message my friends good night.

   Ⓓ Knitting relaxes me.

Goodnight!

You too!

Answer Key

Mostly As: Nature Calls

Just as landscape architect Kotchakorn Voraakhom designs urban areas to coexist with natural elements, you appreciate the natural world and stretch your legs to explore it, one step at a time.

Mostly Bs: Wheely Cool

Strap on your helmet, because nothing's more fun than zipping around the neighborhood on a speedy set of wheels. Anything that has wheels, pedals, or gears motivates you to move! Will you become a cyclist like Alfonsina Strada?

Mostly Cs: Sporty Spirit

Being part of an organized sport (especially with friends) is how you prefer to get your heart pumping. Like soccer star Deyna Castellanos, you have an athletic and competitive spirit that thrives on a team.

Mostly Ds: Variety Pack

Mix it up! What makes you move is learning something new. When rower Sally Kettle was young, she wanted to jump into any challenge. Like Sally, dabbling in a bunch of different activities stimulates your sense of adventure.

Friend Frenzy or Close Circle?

Issa Rae created and starred in a hit TV show that features a close friendship between two women. Sometimes, they hang out with just each other. Other times, they meet up with friends and hang out as a group. What's your friendship style?

The more, the merrier! More friends means more fun.

An acquaintance invites you over to work on a group project together. At her house, what do you do?

Make an effort to get to know her better

Let her lead the conversation. I don't want to seem nosy.

I like meeting new friends as long as I still have time for my crew.

Finish the sentence: A friendship means . . . .

I don't like to spread myself too thin. I like hanging with my besties.

Do you have a nickname for your friend group?

No, my friends are from all over the place.

Yes. (It's based on an inside joke, of course.)

True or false? "My friends know me really well."

True, we spend a lot of time together.

...being there for each other no matter what.

False, most friends do, but not all of them.

...allowing each of us to express ourselves.

You're falling backward into a trust fall! Who do you want to catch you?

My best friends

...having fun together and making memories.

I'll invite my two closest friends for a sleepover.

Someone I know who is also strong

Pick a birthday party scenario.

I'll invite 10 friends to a pizzeria.

Anybody!

SMALLER CIRCLE

In the 1800s, the Brontë sisters encouraged one another to keep writing. You and your friends give each other lots of support too and let everyone just be themselves. If you feel a connection to a new friend, you're open to it.

SOCIAL BALANCER

Having a solid crew is important, but you also like knowing people from different areas of your life. Like Suni Lee working her magic on the beam, managing all your friendships can be a balancing act.

FRIEND FRENZY

Like the friendship app Whitney Wolfe Herd created that helps people make new friends, you love to social network. You're happiest knowing a lot of people and knowing that a lot of people know you!

How Do You Express Your Art?

1. Why do you create art?

   Ⓐ To explore and play with colors and shapes

   Ⓑ To tell captivating stories with exciting themes and rich characters

   Ⓒ To bring a visual journey to life

   Ⓓ To make something tangible from my imagination

2. When she was young, painter Julia López didn't have painting supplies to experiment with. But she was resourceful. She painted on whatever she could find—like paper bags. Which set of materials and equipment draws you in?

   Ⓐ Paint, canvas, paintbrush

   Ⓑ Paper, pencil, computer

   Ⓒ Video camera, microphone, lights

   Ⓓ Clay, carving tools, kiln

3. You're in the kitchen. What sounds like the most fun?

A Adding food coloring to vanilla frosting to make different sugary shades, then spreading it on cupcakes

B Making alphabet veggie soup

C Whipping up a grand meal, with starters, a main course, and a dessert finale!

D Rolling out handmade pasta and cutting it into bite-size pieces

4. Someone is paying you for custom art. What are you creating for them?

A A painted portrait of a pet. Parrot, ferret, goldfish, or cat—I am up for it!

B A written bedtime story for a little kid, who is the main character

C A funny video of friends at a birthday party, edited with music and sounds effects

D A shiny, one-of-a-kind bowl or vase

5. You're staring out the window at a big, old oak tree. What are you thinking?

A How can I mimic the rough texture of the bark with my brushstrokes?

B I am thinking about all the events that took place around the tree over the last century. If only the tree could talk!

C What if I created a time-lapse series of photos of the tree as it ages and looks different throughout an entire year?

D How can I re-create the amazing branches and leaf shapes in clay or wood? The texture would be so cool!

6. Sunday is museum day with your family. Which exhibit will you choose?

A A mural with a social justice message, like the ones Afghan graffiti artist Shamsia Hassani creates

B An exhibit of rare pieces of text, like the notebooks of poet Warsan Shire

C An experimental film—like the ones made by Maya Deren—playing on a blank wall

D Sculptures and artifacts from ancient civilizations—like the ones unearthed by archaeologist Gertrude Bell

Answer Key

Mostly As: Painter's Palette

For you, a blank canvas is an opportunity to project a feeling or vision you have in your imagination using the power of paint. You share a desire to create a connection with the viewer, like Australian painter Judy Cassab did with her award-winning portraits.

Mostly Bs: A Talent for Text

Whether it is writing poetry like Audre Lorde or magicking up new worlds like author Madeleine L'Engle, you use words to represent your artistic spirit. You enrich the page with your unique style of scene setting and character development. What words are you working on now?

Mostly Cs: So Cinematic

Your art is a multisensory experience of visual storytelling. In other words: Movies! Your artistic vision comes to life when you create mood, setting, and dialogue for the screen. One day, you will make your own films and TV shows, like director Ava DuVernay.

Mostly Ds: Clamoring for Clay

Dig in! To the clay, that is. It's your material of choice for carving out your cool 3D concepts. Perhaps you'll make beautiful bowls on a potter's wheel like Nigerian potter Ladi Kwali? The process of using materials like clay to make things with your hands feels natural to you.

COURAGEOUS OR CAUTIOUS?

1. Surfer Maya Gabeira once rode a 73-foot-tall wave—the tallest ever for a female surfer! You've been wanting to take surfing lessons but are scared. It's time to sign up! What are you thinking?

   (A) I'll try. I can always back out if the water is too cold.

   (B) Yes, I'm finally going to do it. I've just got to try.

   (C) I need more time to think. The pit in my stomach is too big.

2. You're at the store with a new friend when you notice that she took a pack of gum from the shelf and slipped it in her pocket. What's your reaction?

   (A) Tell her to put it back. Stealing is not okay.

   (B) Pretend like you didn't see it. You don't want to cause a scene or upset your new friend.

   (C) Ask her why she's stealing the gum

3. You love dogs, but one bit you a few months ago, and now you're hesitant to be around them. How do you get over your fear?

A. Never! (At least not for now.)

B. Give me another few months, and then maybe I'll be ready.

C. Visit a dog rescue shelter, and pet the dogs there.

4. In the early 1900s, Bessie Coleman was a talented airplane pilot who performed stunning tricks in the air. You're about to step onto a plane for the first time for a family trip, and you're feeling super nervous. What do you do?

A. I'd close my eyes and try to sleep the whole time (except for the snack breaks!).

B. I'd grip the armrests for the entire trip, waiting for the plane to land.

C. I'd take some deep breaths, look out the window, and listen to calming music.

5. During her first pageant performance, Nia Franklin impressed the judges with her singing talent. Years later, she was crowned Miss America. Are you ready to show off your singing talent? Auditions for the school musical are tomorrow. Are you going to try out?

A Everyone is nervous at auditions. I know I won't be the only one. So . . . la la la! (That means "yes" in singing.)

B I'm going to need a major pep talk to audition. That's a strong *maybe* for me.

C What if my voice cracks on the high note? I just don't know!

6. When Bana Alabed was seven years old, she used social media to share the story of how her city was being attacked in a war. Would you use your voice to spread awareness about an injustice?

A I don't think so. I wouldn't want the attention.

B If I don't do it, who will? Yes.

C I would, but only as part of a group.

7. At recess, you keep witnessing some older kids being mean to someone in their class. What's your plan?

A I'd tell the adult who is monitoring recess.

B I would walk over and ask the kid if they're okay.

C I would discuss it with my friends, but that's it.

17-21 points

BOUND TO BRAVERY

You feel that true bravery means moving through your fears to accomplish something important to you. Failing and trying again is how you build up your courage. Like Dutch watchmaker Corrie ten Boom, who risked her life to protect Jewish people during World War II, you call upon your courage to help others who need it.

12-16 points

CRAFTING COURAGE

You're really good at listening to your gut and knowing what's right or wrong. But stepping up and taking action can be hard to do. What if you fail or someone gets mad at you? At times, you hold yourself back because of these worries. Courage can grow—just keep practicing it by listening to your truest self!

CAUTION AHEAD

7-11 points

When swimmer Yusra Mardini was escaping her war-torn country, she found herself in a boat with a broken motor that was filling with water. She jumped into the water and helped push the boat to shore. With Yusra as inspiration, take small steps each day to boost up your bravery. What have you been wanting to do but are too scared to try?

What Cause Is Closest to Your Heart?

1. You get to choose a volunteer activity your entire family will participate in. Which one do you pick?

   A Install protective fences for coastal birds nesting on the beach

   B Help organize free yoga sessions for people of all abilities

   C Clean up trash at my local park

   D Put together meals for people who are dealing with food insecurity

2. I support my cause because . . .

   A . . . like animal scientist Temple Grandin says, animals make us human.

   B . . . like blogger Megan Jayne Crabbe knows, there's too much pressure to look a certain way—especially for women and girls.

   C . . . like activist Bernice Notenboom shows in her films, our planet needs our protection.

   D . . . like voting rights advocate María Teresa Kumar knows, there is a lot of justice to keep fighting for.

3. Mother-daughter team Jen and Jordan Reeves are disability advocates. Jordan has a limb difference. One day, she participated in a STEM workshop, where she was asked, "If you could build anything instead of an arm, what would you make?" She built a prosthetic arm in the shape of a unicorn horn that shoots glitter! What invention would you create for a cause?

A Pesticides that don't harm bees and other pollinators

B A line of clothing that celebrates all body types

C A machine that sucks up carbon dioxide from the air to help fight climate change

D Small solar-powered greenhouses that allow people to grow their own food in their backyards or windows inexpensively

4. You're creating a slogan for an issue you care about. Pick one:

A Animals Are People Too

B No One Else Can Be You, So Be Yourself!

C Be a Superhero for Planet Earth

D Rights for All

5. What are some things you do to support your cause?

A I eat less meat.

B I speak up when I hear someone say something unkind about the way another person looks.

C I plant flowers that attract bees or trees that shelter birds.

D I donate part of my allowance to a charity that works to end homelessness and supports human rights.

6. When her tribe's land in the Amazon rain forest was being sold to an oil company, climate activist Nemonte Nenquimo led a group of Waorani people in suing the Ecuadorian government. They won! How would you get others to rally together for a common goal?

A I would host a bake sale fundraiser for a local animal shelter.

B I'd design colorful T-shirts that say, "Being Yourself Is Beautiful."

C I would invite some friends to join me in volunteering at our community garden.

D I could start an after-school club to work on social justice issues. We could organize voter drives, support businesses owned by women of color, and attend protests together.

Answer Key

Mostly As: Cares for Creatures

Marine biologist and author Rachel Carson wrote a book about a silent world, where living things stopped existing because of human destruction. Like Rachel, you feel a sense of urgency to help protect Earth's precious creatures in any way you can!

Mostly Bs: Body Image Booster

Model Clara Holmes uses a wheelchair to get around, but she knows her disability doesn't define her. Inspired by body-positive role models like Clara, you want to spread uplifting messages to people of all shapes, sizes, and abilities.

Mostly Cs: Earth First

You're not okay with humans messing up Mother Nature and will use all your powers of persuasion to push back on climate pollution. Like French activist Lucie Pinson, who worked hard to stop banks from funding dirty coal production, you'll never give up the fight to protect the planet.

Mostly Ds: People's Rights

Cherokee tribal chief Wilma Mankiller fought hard against powerful government forces to restore rights, dignity, and resources to her community. Like Wilma, your heart leads you to stand up for something larger than yourself. Will you change the system from within and become a leader like Wilma?

WHAT KIND OF DOCTOR WOULD YOU BE?

1. You're the friend who is . . .

   Ⓐ . . . great at listening and giving advice.

   Ⓑ . . . doing little experiments out of curiosity.

   Ⓒ . . . good at figuring out solutions to problems.

   Ⓓ . . . not afraid to take care of an injured bird.

2. As a kid growing up in Kenya and Lesotho, zoologist Lucy King loved running free with the farm animals. She played with her dog, rode her pony, and cared for all sorts of critters. Could you do that? What's your stance on animals?

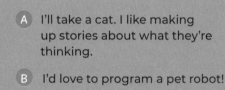

   Ⓐ I'll take a cat. I like making up stories about what they're thinking.

   Ⓑ I'd love to program a pet robot!

   Ⓒ Hmm, I'm more of a dog person. I like long walks, and I give the best belly rubs.

   Ⓓ I'd care for any creature. They're all special.

3. I can see myself . . .

A . . . helping people understand themselves and grow, like psychologist Joy Harden Bradford.

B . . . conducting research in a lab, like quantum physicist Merritt Moore.

C . . . repairing people's bodies, like surgeon Velma Scantlebury.

D . . . caring for an animal's health, like pet wheelchair maker Shaine Kilyun.

4. Which little kids' toy would you still want to play with?

A Not a toy, but I had an imaginary friend I sometimes miss

B My beginner chemistry set

C My doctor's kit. I loved the blood pressure cuff!

D My collection of stuffed animals

5. I like TV shows that . . .

A ... have interesting, complicated characters and story lines.

B ... feature scientific technology, like artificial intelligence.

C ... are medical dramas.

D ... include animals as main characters.

6. Sofia Ionescu-Ogrezeanu was a neurosurgeon who saved lives by performing brain surgeries. What's your scientific superpower?

A Being aware and empathetic

B Thinking beyond what's already known

C Understanding how systems relate to each other

D Tuning in to animal behavior

7. Pick a college major.

A Psychology

B Computer science

C Biology

D Zoology

ANSWER KEY

MOSTLY As: EMOTIONS EXPERT

Your perceptive personality, combined with empathetic energy, would make you a caring doctor, like psychiatrist Elisabeth Kübler-Ross. You give your friends a shoulder to lean on and offer up your ears to listen, making you the resident psychologist!

MOSTLY Bs: LAB LEARNER

Your quest to fine-tune your knowledge will serve you well in a lab setting. You will thrive designing theories, testing them, and running experiments. Maybe you'll invent new medical technology, like biochemist Jennifer Doudna.

MOSTLY Cs: BODY MECHANICS

Overall, you like to understand how things fit together in a system—like how the body works. Your interest in diagnosing problems and coming up with solutions works well for a field in medicine. Will you be a pediatrician, like Nadine Burke Harris?

MOSTLY Ds: ALL ABOUT ANIMALS

You've always had a strong connection to animals, which makes becoming a veterinarian, like Karin Schmidt, a natural fit! Animals would be lucky to have a human like you on their side to protect and heal them.

Precise Person or on the Fly?

Journalist Carolina Guerrero created a popular podcast network featuring Latin American stories told in Spanish. To keep track of all her guests, facts, sources, and stories, she has to be very on top of things! How do you stay organized when completing a big assignment?

I dive in and figure it out as I go.

At a modern art museum, which kind of painting draws your eye?

Splattered canvases

Geometric shapes

I try to break the work into smaller chunks, so I don't get overwhelmed.

You're making cookies! What's your baking style?

I keep a calendar of what I need to do every day and how to do it.

What's inside your backpack?

Everything possible. Who knows what I'll need?

Notebooks, pencil case, schedule, snack bag

Last week, you had a box of 100 crayons. How many are in there now?

Still 100, arranged by color in rainbow order

Gather all the ingredients, bowls, and measuring tools before starting

Grab what I need as I go through the recipe

Guesstimate the measurements

Pick a job.

Improv teacher

Airline pilot

Your birthday is coming up. How do you approach party planning?

How am I supposed to know that?!

I'll create a website with all the details and an RSVP list.

I'll tell my friends to hold the date and then figure out the plan later.

The day before, I'll casually invite a group to come over.

WHAT KIND OF BIRTHDAY BASH SHOULD YOU HAVE?

1. Do you prefer doing activities with lots of friends or just a few? What's your ideal group size?

   A A smaller group, so it's not so loud

   B A big crew having lots of wild fun!

   C Just a few friends, so we can have a cozy hang

   D A medium-size bunch works for me—enough people to have variety, but not so many that it is overwhelming

2. Shortly before her 80th birthday, explorer Barbara Hillary trekked to the South Pole. Are you up for a birthday adventure?

   A I'll stick a little closer to home. How about a nature walk?

   B Yes! How about rock climbing, like boulderer Miho Nonaka?

   C Hmm, I'd rather explore relaxation.

   D I'd be into a mental adventure.

3. Equestrian Tegan Vincent-Cooke first started riding horses as a hobby, and now she's training for the Paralympics. What's a hobby you'd like to delve into?

   A Making mosaics out of bits of shimmery glass

   B Gymnastics

   C Mixing up my own beauty products using household ingredients

   D Playing board games with clever clues to solve

4. Which scenario sounds like a good time?

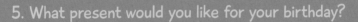

A Four friends at a craft studio making jewelry

B Twenty buddies playing laser tag

C Having two of my besties over for a beauty spa day, movies, and a sleepover

D Ten pals figuring out "Who done it?" at a murder mystery party.

5. What present would you like for your birthday?

A A chocolate mold set, so I can make my own treats

B A yearlong pass at a trampoline park

C A soapmaking kit

D The newest book from my favorite detective series

6. You're walking around your town's shopping district with a few friends. Which stores are you popping into?

A The art supply store

B The video game arcade

C The nail salon for a pedicure

D The toy store to look at spy kits

7. Pick a vibe.

A Arty

B Active

C Glamorous

D Mysterious

ANSWER KEY

MOSTLY As: MAKER MAGIC

Isatou Ceesay worked with local women to make jewelry out of materials that people had thrown away. (Don't worry—they clean them first!) Like Isatou, you have a can-do crafting spirit. Gather your friends for an art party where you can exercise your imagination and celebrate at the same time. And the best part? Your friends get to take their creations home.

MOSTLY Bs: SPORTY CELEBRATION

Game on! You love the adrenaline rush of racing around and competing with your crew. Whether you're tackling an obstacle course or hitting the bowling alley like bowler Clara Juliana Guerrero Londoño, your birthday is sure to be a bona fide blast. Save some energy for blowing out your candles!

MOSTLY Cs: PAMPERING PARTY

Ready to relax? With your love of playing with potions and lotions, the ultimate spa day with your closest friends sounds like the perfect birthday outing for you. Like beauty brand owner Rihanna says, "Makeup is there for you to have fun with." And you totally agree!

MOSTLY Ds: GUESSING GAME

Solving puzzles and cracking clues stimulate your strategic mind. Teaming up with your buds to bust out of an escape room would be an entertaining way to celebrate your birthday! Did you know that Supreme Court Justice Sonia Sotomayor wanted to be a detective when she was younger?

What Sport Suits You Best?

1. Merlene Joyce Ottey broke a record for indoor track and field when she ran the 200-meter dash in less than 22 seconds. She's always racing against the clock. Do you like playing sports that use time pressure as part of the competition?

   A No

   B Yes, timing sets apart the amateurs from the pros!

   C I don't mind it—timing keeps me focused.

   D As long as it's more about the entire game being timed and not each move

2. Do you want to wear special footwear and clothes made just for your sport?

   A Yes, it's fun to show off my personality with athletic gear.

   B Sure, I'll wear a pair of sleek sneakers.

   C No, I just want to wear whatever makes me feel confident.

   D Yes, I want to wear a team uniform with my name and number on it.

3. What's a trait you are proud of?

A Agility, like when Serena Williams darts around the tennis court

B Speed, like when Allyson Felix sprints around the track

C Strategy, like when Phiona Mutesi plays chess

D Precision, like when Megan Rapinoe kicks a soccer ball into the goal

4. Do you like playing sports that use balls?

A Yes, but I like other equipment too

B No

C Not really

D Definitely

5. Doreen Simmons was a sports commentator who became an expert at discussing sumo wrestling in Japan. What might a commentator say watching your favorite sport?

A Powerful serve!

B She's beating her own record!

C Whoa, genius move!

D That's some fancy footwork!

6. On a scale of 1 to 10 (where 1=Don't Break a Sweat and 10=Drenched), how active do you like to be with sports?

A Between 2 and 10—I bounce back and forth.

B I'm a 10! I like being fast!

C Somewhere between 1 and 4—I'm more into brain games.

D I like the range from 5 to 9. I like running around a field, keeping up with the action.

7. Weightlifter Amna Al Haddad said, "No matter what the challenges are, never walk away from your dream." How do you psych yourself up for a challenge?

A I tell myself I'm strong, inside and out.

B I dance around my room like crazy.

C Plan! I start by figuring out each step of what I need to do to meet my goal.

D The support of my good friends cheers me on.

Answer Key

Mostly As: Team Tennis

Are you ready to hit the court? You're good at thinking on your feet, and you have oodles of energy—both great qualities for tennis. Like tennis superstar Billie Jean King, who played with passion and incredible skill, you would bring your best to the game—and have fun too!

Mostly Bs: Run Fun

Time to lace up your sneakers. You were born to run! With your need for speed and drive to achieve your personal best, clocking laps around the track could be the perfect sport for you. Like Paralympian Fleur Jong, you race toward the finish line with determination.

Mostly Cs: Chess Champ

Checkmate! Your strategic, mathematical mind is made for a stimulating one-on-one sport like chess. You might like giving your brain a workout with the advanced planning and quick thinking chess requires. When she was 15, Susan Polgar was the best female chess player in the world. What's your next move?

Mostly Ds: Soccer-Ready

You've got team spirit and like being active with your buddies, which makes soccer a super sport for you. As soccer referee Jawahir Jewels Roble knows, the game demands high energy, strategy, and control on the field. With your enthusiasm and practice, get ready to block shots and have a blast!

How Do You Make Music?

1. At a very young age, musician Hazel Scott already knew she had an amazing ear for music. She could play the piano just by listening to the notes. What do you pay attention to most when you listen to music?

   A The lyrics and the voice

   B The melody

   C Which instruments are being played

   D The rhythm

2. When you're hanging out in your room listening to music, what else are you doing?

   A Singing in the mirror (with a hairbrush as a microphone, naturally)

   B Jamming on the air guitar

   C Lying on my bed and letting songs wash over me

   D Tapping on my desk, with pencils for drumsticks

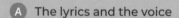

3. Opera singer Maria Callas captured the hearts of her audience when she performed in famous operas like *Norma*, *La Traviata*, and *Tosca*. She shined onstage. Imagine this: You and your friends are writing a pop music opera. Which part are you in charge of?

A. Writing the words for the songs and singing

B. Playing electric guitar

C. Writing the music and making sure it all sounds good together

D. Keeping the beat on the drums

4. Mata Hari was the stage name of a dancer who entertained her fans with bedazzled outfits and eye-catching moves. What would your stage name be?

A. MC Word Whiz

B. String Shredder

C. The Captain

D. The Beatkeeper

5. You're walking in the woods on a beautiful day. What are you noticing?

A The sounds of the songbirds

B The intricate spiderwebs in the tall grass and trees

C How all the forest noises blend perfectly to make nature's song

D The even pace of my footsteps crunching the leaves below

6. Your teacher assigns everyone a classroom job. Pick one.

A Making announcements

B Choosing a dance video for everyone to follow during an energizing break

C Taking attendance

D Setting the timer for quiet reading

7. When you are scrolling through radio stations, what sounds make you stop and listen?

A A song with a compelling voice and words, like how Beyoncé sings

B A tune with a powerful guitar solo, like how Joan Jett rocks out

C Classical music, like the orchestras Freida Belinfante conducted

D Cool drumbeats, like the ones Nandi Bushell bangs out

Answer Key

Mostly As: Sing Your Heart Out

Warm up your vocals because belting out lyrics is how you express your musical magic. Sometimes you even write your own! Whether it's in the shower or on stage like rapper MC Soffia, your voice is your instrument. What's your latest song about?

Mostly Bs: Guitar Star

For you, music is all about melodies—and the invigorating sound of the guitar gets you into the groove. Rosetta Tharpe energized the crowd with her soulful six-string strumming. Which notes will you pluck to perfect your sound?

Mostly Cs: Confident Conductor

Orchestra conductors, like Xian Zhang, make sure all the instruments are played at the right time with the right audio level. Your keen ear for how different instruments layer and mix to create a unique sound would make conducting an excellent choice for you!

Mostly Ds: Drumroll, Please!

There's something about the steady beat of a drum that stirs up your excitement and emotion. Playing the drums requires excellent coordination and precise timing—two things you've totally got. Maybe you'll bang on a bongo like divine drummer Millo Castro Zaldarriaga. *Ba ba boom! Ba ba boom!*

Illustration Credits

6: Amanda Hall. 7: Amari Mitnaul. 8: Vanessa Lovegrove. 11: Lydia Mba. 12: Claudia Carieri (Curie), Bhavna Madan (Gupta). 13: Lisa Lanoë (Matsuoka), Maya Ealey (Imafidon). 14: Maïté Franchi. 15: Valencia Spates (Butler), Lily Kim Qian (Kwan), Eline Van Dam (Madonna). 16: Paola Rollo. 18: Jeanetta Gonzales (Carter), Keisha Morris (León). 19: Marta Signori (Loren), T.S. Abe (Chapman). 21: Adriana Bellet. 22: Marta Signori (Hepburn), Sophia Martineck (Austen). 23: Ronique Ellis (Ulmer), Marta Signori (Callas), Katerina Voronina (Thunberg), Zara Picken (Bly). 24: Lisa Lanoë. 25: Ana Juan (O'Keeffe), Keisha Okafor (Martin), Sarah Loulendo (Power). 26: Eline Van Dam. 27: Keturah Ariel. 28: Renike (Jamison), Thandiwe Tshabalala (Angelou). 29: Claudia Carieri (Makosinski), Camilla Ru (Williams). 30: Sally Nixon. 31: Camille de Cussac. 32: Paola Rollo (Khan), Alexandra Bowman (Stanley). 33: Jui Talukder. 34: Olivia Fields (Chisholm), Sol Cotti (Titmus). 35: Taylor McManus (Canady), Elisabetta Stoinich (Lovelace). 36: Sara Olmos. 37: Giulia Tomai (Cristoforetti), Sarah Loulendo (Empinotti), Kate Prior (Fiolek). 38: Thaiz Zafalon. 39: Pau Zamro. 40: Sarah Madden. 41: Karyn Lee (Arora), Jui Talukder (Barman), Michelle D'Urbano (Rabana), Salini Perera (Lee). 42: Kylie Akia Erwin. 43: Helen Li (Guy-Blaché), Annalisa Ventura (da Silva). 44: Eleni Debo. 46: Kasia Bogdańska. 47: Caribay MB. 49: Aisha Akeju. 50: Ping Zhu (Copeland), Sharee Miller (Bushell). 51: Salini Perera (Raisman), Tyla Mason (Baker). 52: Noa Snir. 53: Bodil Jane. 54: Thandiwe Tshabalala (Maathai), Elisa Seitzinger (von Fürstenberg). 55: Priya Kuriyan (Malavath), Jonell Joshua (Jeters), Andressa Meissner (Malaviya), Cristina Spanò (Montessori). 57: Jennifer M. Potter (Andrews and Walton Hamilton), Sara Bondi (Yousafzai). 58: Noa Denmon. 59: Nicole Miles. 60: Barbara Dziadosz (Child), Justine Lecouffe (Lindgren). 61: Annalisa Ventura (Seacole), Giulia Tomai (Christie). 62: Pau Zamro. 63: Sarah Loulendo. 64: Emmanuelle Walker. 66: Fanesha Fabre. 67: Anna Dixon. 68: Kathrin Honesta. 69: Marta Signori (Lamarr), Alleanna Harris (Kalema-Zikusoka), Marylou Faure (Baret), Cristina Amodeo (Perón). 70: Giorgia Marras. 71: Geraldine Sy (Nordblad), Naomi Anderson-Subryan (Govera), Kelsee Thomas (Burns). 73: Barbara Dziadosz. 75: Irene Rinaldi. 76: Martina Paukova (Krafft), Geraldine Sy (Gurib-Fakim). 77: Sally Caulwell (Ocampo-Friedmann), Marijke Buurlage (Procter). 78: Fabiola Aldrete. 79: Lily Nie (Chen), Jo Zixuan (Perkins). 80: Marina Venancio. 81: Jennifer M. Potter. 82: Tatsiana Burgaud (Sakkhija), Olivia Fields (Hamilton). 83: Cindy Echevarria (Soto-Innes), Lily Nie (Hu). 84: Josefina Preumayr. 85: Alice Barberini. 89: Sally Deng. 90: Kamo Frank. 91: Ana Juan. 92: Taylor McManus (Insooni), Anine Bösenberg (McEwans). 93: Lisk Feng (Luo), Martina Paukova (Anning). 94: Debora Guidi. 95: Akvile Magicdust (Corr), Debora Guidi (DePrince), Onyinye Iwu (Mutesi). 96: Anastasia Magloire Williams. 97: Meel Tamphanon (Wintour), DeAndra Hodge (Sullivans). 98: Auréelia Durand (Gebru), Sarah Wilkins (Cholita Climbers). 99: Paola Rollo (Heaney), Alice Barberini (Burgess, Troop 6000), Jennifer Berglund (El Kott Helander), Kathrin Honesta (Watson). 100: Johnalynn Holland. 101: Eleni Kalorkoti. 102: Noa Snir. 103: Eleni Kalorkoti. 104: Gabrielle Tesfaye (Betul), Ping Zhu (Cruz). 105: Naki Narh (Johnson), Jeanne Detallante (Newby-Fraser). 106: Mia Saine (Urrutia), Helen Li (Fukuda). 108: Kate Prior. 109: Xuan Loc Xuan (Voraakhom), Cristina Portolano (Strada), Sol Cotti (Castellanos), Sonia Pulido (Kettle). 110: Naomi Silverio. 111: Anna Dixon (Herd), Danielle Elysse Mann (Lee), Elisabetta Stoinich (Brönte Sisters). 112: Acacia Rodriguez. 114: Cristina Portolano. 115: Cecilia Puglesi (Cassab), Kelsee Thomas (Lorde), Adesewa Adekoya (DuVernay), Sarah Madden (Kwali). 116: Martina Paukova. 117: Toni D. Chambers. 118: Tatheer Syeda. 120: Beatrice Cerocchi. 121: Bárbara Tamilin. 122: Sofía Acosta-Verea (Nenquimo). 123: Sarah Wilkins (Carson), Trudi-Ann Hemans (Holmes), Sarah Loulendo (Pinson), Alexandra Bowman (Mankiller). 124: Jennifer M. Potter. 125: Irene Rinaldi. 126: Elenia Beretta. 127: Jennifer M. Potter (Kübler-Ross), Irene Rinaldi (Doudna), Veronica Carratello (Harris), Elenia Beretta (Schmidt). 128: Noa Denmon. 129: Camilla Perkins (Ochoa), Maïté Franchi (Cauffman), Fanesha Fabre (Shanté). 131: DeAndra Hodge (Cooke) 133: Naki Narh (Ceesay), Amalteia (Londoño), Jestenia Southerland (Rihanna), Kathrin Honesta (Sotomayor). 134: Luisa Rivera. 135: Kim Holt (Rapinoe), Petra Braun (Simmons). 136: Eline Van Dam. 137: Emmanuelle Walker (King), Mia Saine (Jong), Elenia Beretta (Polgar), Veronica Ruffato (Roble). 138: Sabrena Khadija. 139: Monica Garwood. 140: Gosia Herba. 141: Keisha Okafor (MC Soffia), Aisha Akeju (Tharpe), Ping Zhu (Zhang), Sarah Wilkins (Zaldarriaga).